Before Rea

The book you are holding contains a few of the most vulnerable moments in my life. I was hesitant to reveal the dark moments of my past as I was afraid of what people might think. The thought of being judged for the decisions and choices I have made paralyzed me into a state of silence. Many may not agree with my willingness to be so open. However, my hope is that by being candid with regard to my darkest moments will help others see how the light of Christ guided me back to Him. In the book of Ruth, we read that suffering and despair led Ruth to her redeemer. In the same way, I believe suffering led me to my Lord and can lead you to Him as well. In Acts 17, Paul writes that God is not far from us, and that He has placed us where are in the world to feel our way towards Him. I am paraphrasing, but perhaps God needs us to feel weakness so we return to Him for strength. No matter what you are going through, you are aloud to feel sad, but I plead with you not to stay there. I am writing this in hopes that you are inspired to take action and start living the way He wants you to live. I pray that you are open to the challenge of digging deep into God's word. My hope is that you will discover the dryness of your soul and discover the soul quenching solution that He has to offer.

Acknowledgments

As I watched my mother take her last breath, my eyes were opened to the truth of the writings in James *"For you are a mist that appears for a little time and then vanishes..."* (James 4:14). I realized how short our time on earth is and began to question everything. Through the journey of questioning my faith, I discovered the truth of the gospel. Though I miss her so much, I have confidence knowing that I will see her again. I dedicate this book to my beautiful mother and her patience with me. I am so thankful for her constant prayers that I would one day be added to the Lord's kingdom. I also want to express gratitude to my loving husband Luke, who constantly encouraged me to write this. Finally, I would like to thank my Aunt Tami, who not only spent her sweet time editing this book, but patiently guided and helped me on my path towards living for Christ.

Foreword

I was raised in the church and questioned little with regard to His church. My grandparents were in the church. My parents and siblings were in the church. My dad served as an elder and my mom served as a Bible class teacher. Being apart of His church was a way of life and took precedence over everything. From an early age, I read the Bible through most of my years. This was not necessarily by choice but out of a desire to please my father's request that I complete this task. I began teaching Bible classes from a young age as well, which would force me into His word, and again I did not question my duty in doing so.

My niece, Megan, was brought into the church at an early age when her mother met my brother. This little girl questioned everything about the church. Frankly, I ignored my part of helping to mold her. That was her parents' job in my mind. However, when Megan, about a month after her mother's death asked me a question about the Bible and how to study, I was at a loss at what she even meant. She had been baptized at the age of 16 at church camp. I just assumed everyone in the church read the Bible and studied His word, and that it was their own personal job to complete. I remember standing in the hallway of my brother's home praying for help to be able to get through to her in the weekend I was there for a short visit.

Prior to this visit, I had been ordering

copies of the book, A Muscle and a Shovel, and providing a copy to anyone willing to read it. In this quest, I gave every family member a copy. I felt this book not only great resource for converting others to the church, but also great for those within the church who from time to time need vindication for their belief. As I was packing up my brother's home for a move, we came across the copy I had given to Megan's mom and dad. It was perfect, I would have her begin with this book – a starting place I could work with from Georgia!

Megan was receptive and from then on, I was fielding millions of questions. This forced me to study deeper and be able to explain what God intended for her to know. I welcomed the opportunity since I felt this was one thing I could do for her mother, Jill. I intended to be sure that Megan would one day be united with her mother again.

Parched takes you on Megan's self-reflective journey into His word. My prayer is that this book will prick your heart and lead you deeper into a relationship with our Lord and Savior, Jesus Christ. Megan's heart was pricked by her willingness to dive into the word.

Ironically, Megan now serves as my inspiration. I am humbled at her honest grace. I am humbled at how easily she interacts with people as she invites everyone to hear His word. She accepts no excuses. She accepts all situations and will work with anyone with a heart to learn about Jesus. She challenges me to be a better soldier in the kingdom. She will challenge you as well. -Tamera H

Table of Contents

"So Paul, standing in the midst of the Areopagus, said: "Men of Athens, I perceive that in every way you are very religious. For as I passed along and observed the objects of your worship, I found also an altar with this inscription: To the unknown god.' What therefore you worship as unknown, this I proclaim to you. The God who made the world and everything in it, being Lord of heaven and earth, does not live in temples made by man, nor is he served by human hands, as though he needed anything, since he himself gives to all mankind life and breath and everything. And he made from one man every nation of mankind to live on all the face of the earth, having determined allotted periods and the boundaries of their dwelling place, that they should seek God, and perhaps feel their way toward him and find him. Yet he is actually not far from each one of us..." Acts 17:22-27

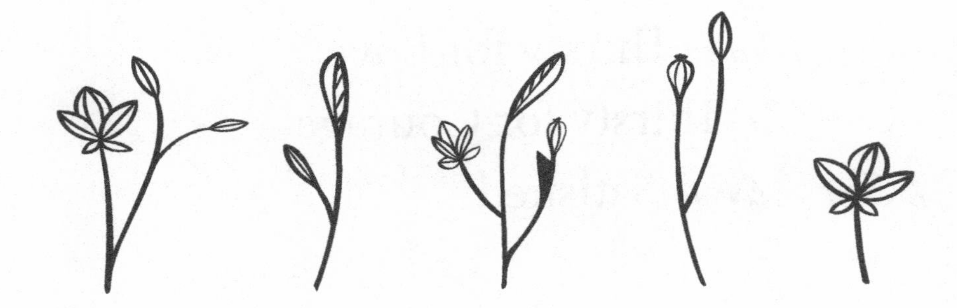

Introduction

One of the many times I accompanied my mother in the hospital, she was not allowed to eat or drink due to an upcoming procedure. Her mouth was so dry that her lips would crack. She longed for a sip of water but was not allowed to have it. I remember wanting to help her be more comfortable, so I walked to the nurse's station and asked what I could do to help the dryness of her mouth. The nurse gave me pink mouth swabs and told me to dip them in water to moisten her mouth. She was refreshed by the smallest amount of water from those swabs. In the same way water provided refreshment for my mother, I feel God's word is able to refresh our souls. Just like my mother's dry cracking lips, my soul once felt as if it was dry and cracking. It felt as if I could crack into a million pieces at any moment. I longed for a soul satisfying solution that I was not sure existed.

When children are outside playing, they often forget to come inside and drink water. The distraction of fun keeps them preoccupied from their body feeling thirsty. Once they realize their thirst, they may walk into the house and pick something that is unhealthy for them, such as coca cola. Instead of hydrating themselves with water, they end up more thirsty because coca cola is a diuretic. Although bad for them, it tastes good. I was a lot like those children. I was distracted by all the fun around me that it caused me to neglect my dehydrated soul.

Once I realized my thirst, I often dabbled in solutions that were bad for me or drank substances that did not contain nutritional sustenance. This left me feeling parched and longing for a solution I could not put my finger on. *Thirst* is a synonym for a strong desire or craving for something (Keathley, 2004).

Are you thirsty? I am not referring to the physical thirst that is forced before a procedure due to not being allowed to eat or drink. Nor is it thirst experienced after eating ice cream, or returning from a long run. The thirst I am referring to is the deep longing thirst within your soul. This type of thirst is described by the Psalmist who wrote: "*As a deer longs for flowing streams, so my soul longs for you, O God. My soul thirsts for God, for the living God.*" (Psalm 42:1-2).

Quite possibly, you are like the child outside playing that has not fully realized that you are thirsty because you have been preoccupied with fun. Since I was like that child, I wanted to write to women who feel or felt like me. My thoughts are being directed toward the woman who feels like there is a deep thirst within her soul that she cannot quench. These reflections are also for the women who have not yet discovered that thirst. I am striving to reach the ones who have a deep longing for something they cannot quite put their finger on, but are aware that there is something missing in their lives.

I know I cannot be the only one who has questioned if there is more to life than merely growing old and dying. I cannot possibly be the only one surrounded by loved ones, but still left feeling lonely at times. I cannot be the only one who never thought that death could affect my life because I was living in a state of comfortable ignorance. I cannot be the only one who was surviving off of physical substances that left me feeling empty. Nor can I be the only one who desired a soul quenching close-knit relationship with God and His people, but did not know where to begin to establish this type of relationship. I am going to go out on a limb here and guess that maybe you feel this, too?

If you can relate to any of these scenarios, then I hope you will benefit from this book. I have written this in hopes that someone out there with a weary, parched soul will be quenched as mine was. If that is you, as you refresh your soul with this reading, I invite you to answer the soul quenching questions at the end of each chapter.

I am convinced that God has placed this thirst in our souls, so that we will long for Him. In our search to quench this thirst, we will discover His church. Once we are satisfied, we are compelled to tell others about it. Which then results in each of us bursting someone's bubble of contentment.

Before we get to how I arrived at that conclusion, I would like you to do some self-inspection. I spent four years of my life trying to discover who I was, who God is, and what He wants from me. It was the best thing I did for myself. Many of my girlfriends tell me they want the peace I have, but they do not know where to start. The truth is, there is no good place to start, the secret is to just decide to take action.

Instead of remaining in a safe place and pretending like I have my life together and always have, I am going to expose myself in this book. I am going to share journal entries that contain moments when I was extremely emotionally drained and longing for a solution but searched in all the wrong places. I have prayed for guidance, and I am jumping out and letting the light shine in my dark stagnant places.

Before reading further, write out your struggles and doubts in this section of the book. List your thirsty places. Reveal your thirst, so we can move forward. Whatever it is, acknowledge it, acknowledge that you cannot conquer it alone. If you are having a hard time discovering your thirsty places, examine your life and how you spend your free time. Is there a chance you are too full on the things the world has to offer? What are some things you want to hold on to that are preventing you from learning more about Christianity? Pause your reading and nourish your soul with some therapeutic writing.

Here is an example of things I was once Thirsty for:

Attention

Purpose

A Relationship

Closure

Time

Significance

Comfort

I am thirsty for: ______________________________

____

This thirst has caused me to ______________________________

____

______________________________ is holding me back.

I am too full on ______________________________

____

I spend my free time ______________________________

____

I am ready to ______________________________

____

Week One: Parched

Jesus said to them, "I am the bread of life; he who comes to Me will not hunger, and he who believes in Me will never thirst." John 3:35

As I sit here and write this chapter of this book, I have one drain in each of my sides from a procedure called a mastectomy. These drains are removing extra fluid from my chest cavity. I am on disability from my job as a nurse for the next few months as I start chemotherapy because I have been diagnosed with breast cancer. This may sound sad to you, and sometimes I feel the despair and unfairness creep in and take hold of my emotions. However, I feel closer with God than I have in years. If you are wondering how I can boldly say that cancer has brought me closer to God, I hope that curiosity causes you to keep reading.

I believe a diagnosis of cancer is similar to Christianity in some ways. Inside my body, I have this deadly bundle of cells, hiding and growing rapidly, however, as of now, I feel healthy. The cancer is isolated into one tumor. I could choose to not have chemotherapy because I feel just fine, ignoring the cells left behind after surgery. I could continue ignoring the fact that I have this disease, and live as long as I can until it starts multiplying and kills me. This sounds like a pretty compelling plan considering the fact that chemotherapy will leave me bald, vulnerable, and cause me to have a low immune system. Plus, I am completely ignorant about the whole process. Besides, who has time to be ignorant, hurt, sick, or vulnerable?

I could choose to stay in that state of ignorance, because that is where it feels safe. Ignoring this disease would be easy enough to do. But there is only so long I can do that because eventually, if left untreated, my triple negative breast cancer will multiply and spread and result in my death. How do I know this? This was knowledge gained after listening to my doctors who specialize in oncology and researching this type of disease on my own. Once I was no longer ignorant about the treatment I needed for my special type of cancer, I felt compelled to go through with the chemotherapy. I could no longer ignore my cancer.

Compared to cancer, I believe the sin in my life once functioned in the same manner. Often times, I felt perfectly fine while sinning. At one time it became easy to hide and ignore because I refused to learn about it. When I approached the Bible and my sin was exposed, I wanted to shut it because it made me feel vulnerable. Once I learned of my sin, I had a choice to make: pursue a solution, or remain in a state of ignorance and let it one day result in my spiritual death.

I think one of Satan's greatest tactics is to keep us ignorant. He convinces us that we are fulfilled without having to be obedient to God. He makes living the Christian life look silly and unappealing because there are so many "rules." He keeps us away from the Bible because He convinces us it is outdated or that we are unable to understand it. He keeps us from the church because He convinces us the people in it are hypocrites. He persuades us to seek out self-help and inspirational books instead of the Bible. He tricks us into thinking it is okay to stay outside of Christ because our time on earth is endless. I think the best tactic he uses, is Biblical ignorance.

One writer put it this way:

"When women grow increasingly lax in their pursuit of Bible literacy, everyone in their circle of influence is affected. Rather than acting as salt and light, we become bland contributions to the environment we inhabit and shape, indistinguishable from those who have never been changed by the gospel. Home, church, community, and country desperately need the influence of women who know why they believe what they believe, grounded in the Word of God. They desperately need the influence of women who love deeply and actively the God proclaimed in the Bible. "Jen Wilkens

We have a book that is inspired and able to rid of us our thirsts and provide us encouragement. But Satan keeps us away from it from it by keeping us ignorant. Instead of turning to scripture for comfort and spending our lives learning about God and

His desires, Satan keeps us content with chasing our own desires and looking at the Bible as if it is irrelevant. My life is a reflection of these truths. I failed to see the inspiration of God's word. I dabbled in the solutions of this world and my cup ran dry. I became so spiritually dehydrated that it almost resulted in my spiritual death. But I escaped his false sense of security and my prayer is that this book helps you escape too.

For the longest time, I called myself a Christian, but I was ignorant in regards to the true meaning of Christianity. I believed in my own, made up version of God. Once I found out about the God of the Bible, I was convicted to keep learning. I began to realize that I was never fully dedicated to living for Him because I did not truly know what He wanted for my life. I was convinced that Christianity was boring and judgmental. Why would I want to be dedicated to a life that seemed so judgmental and filled with things I was not allowed to do? I wanted the title of being a Christian, but I also wanted to live my life with no restrictions.

But then cancer came along and changed my whole perspective. I watched my mother take her last breath and I began to question everything. Life seemed fleeting. I began to wonder if anything truly lasts. I was so thirsty for answers. Once I was in the church, I almost died to pride and contentment due to these causing me to hide my dried out, stagnant places that were causing my soul to mold and rot. I was refusing to let God replenish those places because I refused to reveal them.

It was not until I fully dedicated my life to understanding the word of God, being more open about my struggles, and becoming more active in His church that I finally discovered the solution to my thirst. Once my perspective changed, cancer became a blessing to me. Although both times (with mom and now me) it has been a long process, I am thankful for it. Without cancer, life would have remained comfortable and too busy to grow as a Christian. I would have never realized that my Christianity was based purely on my feelings and not on the stable foundation of the word of God. I would have never had time to write this book, see God's church in action, or be forced to dig deep in times of distress.

Being plagued with breast cancer and losing my mother all by the age of 28 was not on my to-do list. But through these trials, I was comforted by God's word and I discovered Christ and the soul satisfying solution that being apart of His church offers, and I am excited to share my journey with you.

So let's get started. I do not know your background or if you have ever even opened a Bible, but in this moment, I want you to pause and jump in. I want you to start by reading the book of Ruth. It helped me gain a new perspective on suffering, so I thought this would be a good place to start.

Pause and read the book of Ruth. It is found in the Old Testament.

In the first chapter of this book, we read of the death of three Ephrathites from Bethlehem in Judah: Elimelech, Mahlon and Chilion. These deaths turned three women into widows. We might read this and wonder, why did God let all of this happen? Is that not pointless suffering? But if we look into this deeper we read that this may have been the result of the actions of Naomi's husband Elimelech. During the days when the Judges ruled, there was a famine in the land. Instead of looking to God for help during the famine, Elimelech chose to seek help in the godless country of Moab. He turned away from God and ended up dying. Instead of remaining in Moab after the death of Elimelech, his wife Naomi picked herself up from the hurt and decided to return to Bethlehem because she *"had heard in the fields of Moab that the LORD had visited his people and given them food"* (Ruth 1:6). Ruth, could have chosen to go back with Orpah, but her love and devotion to Naomi, caused her to be blessed in the end.

When I read this passage, I was reminded of Paul's words in Acts 17:24-25

"The God who made the world and everything in it, being Lord of heaven and earth, does not live in temples made by man, nor is he served by human hands, as though he needed anything, since he himself gives to all mankind life and breath and everything. And he made from one man every nation of mankind to live on all the face of the earth, having determined allotted periods and the boundaries of their dwelling place, that they should seek God, and perhaps feel their way toward him and find him. Yet he is actually not far from each one of us."

This shows that God has granted us free will and placed each of us where we are meant to be in order to feel our way towards Him. This proved true in the book of Ruth. This also proves true in my life. Reflecting on my life, I realized the truth of these verses. I was born in Oklahoma, but because of my biological father's choices, my mom was forced to raise me as a single mother. When my mom met and dated the man who would become my actual father, he moved us to Ohio where they were married. In Ohio, I was exposed to the constant light of Christ. For example, I was blessed with godly grandparents who prayed with me at night and ensured I was in Bible class and attended church camp during the summer. I was blessed with family members and church members who introduced me to the gospel. I was exposed to the light, but I had a choice to make; I could choose to follow the light, learn more about why my grandparents and others followed the teachings of the Bible or I could ignore it and turn away.

God gave me a chance and an opportunity to feel my way towards Him by the events that happened in my life and honestly

I turned away and refused for a while, which introduced the constant thirst into my life. However, once I chose to seek God and learn what He wanted from me through His word, my whole life changed.

Sure I was sad and torn when I had to leave my Oklahoma family, but what if I had stayed? Would I have obeyed the gospel? When my mom passed, if I were not in Ohio with godly influence, would I have remained a Christian? I do not believe so. I believe Oklahoma may have been my Moab. Like Naomi, my mother chose to take action and move us to Bethlehem (Ohio). My mother's suffering led her to her Bethlehem. My suffering forced me out of my Moab (the party scene) and into Bethlehem (the Christian life). What about you? Figuratively speaking of course, are you in Moab? Or on your way to Bethlehem?

In my dark place, (Let's call it my Moab); I was faced with two options: One option was to search for a light. The other was to play the victim of my circumstances, continue dwelling in the darkness, and feeling sorry for myself after my mom died. The first option was more painful and difficult, but has proven to be worth it.

By now you should have written out your thirsty places as I told you to in the previous chapter. Doing so may be hard, but please do not skip this part. Reflecting on how we ended up in our thirsty places helps gain insight to Acts 17. It is amazing to reflect on the events that occur in our lives and see that God placed us where we are and has exposed Himself at least once through someone else and we most likely ignored it.

When I think about past events that have left a dent in my life, sometimes it is easy to still become bitter and start picking up imaginary bricks to hand build my crumbled walls into tall, sturdy thick walls. Bitterness creeps in and begins to turn into numbness again and it becomes tempting to turn into a clam and push people away. But then I find those feelings melting away when I start wondering, what if God lets us journey through painful experiences so that we realize only He can save us? What if His desire is that these experiences soften our hearts and expose our weaknesses so we can understand His strength and then radiate that strength to others?

We cannot radiate through hand built walls. We cannot return to Bethlehem if we refuse to leave our Moab. If you are numb from going through hurtful experiences one too many times, my prayer is that your walls will be torn down and that your heart will be softened. If you are fearful to leave your Moab, my prayer is that you are able to conquer that fear with faith and become courageous enough to tell your story to help someone. Your story could be the key that unlocks someone else's prison.

The following chapters of this book will be a reflection of the things I went through in my version of Moab. Each chapter will contain a thirst I had in my life, and a solution I found in God's word. My prayer is that it inspires you to dig deep into the Bible and learn about God and His plan for your life. This is a book to encourage you to look to God's word for fulfillment.

Thirst Quenching Questions

Do you believe in God's word? Why or Why not?

Read Matthew 24:35; what does this tell us about God's words?

Read Hebrews 4:12-13; what does this tell us about God's word?

Read 2 Timothy 3:16-17; What is scripture given to us for?

What do you currently use scripture for?

What is your current way of studying scripture?

Who is God to you?

What is faith?

Read Jeremiah 17:9; what does this tell us about our heart?

Is your faith based purely on what you feel in your heart?

Read Romans 10:17; how does this define faith?

What is your relationship with the word of God?

Reflect on where you have been placed in life, are you in Moab, or on your way to Bethlehem?

Week Two: Thirsty in the Wilderness

"O God, you are my God; earnestly I seek you;
my soul thirsts for you; my flesh faints for you,
as in a dry and weary land where there is no water."

Psalm 63:1

My heart skips a beat each time I have a flashback to a moment when my mom was still alive. A simple smell, sound, or song can often do the trick. In this moment, writing about my experience with being thirsty in my own wilderness has me in full on flashback mode.

I am taken back to 2013 when I had to accompany mom to the hospital. I can still hear her sweet tone of voice while she was waiting on me to park the car and join her in the emergency room. As I was walking down the hall to the admissions desk and rounded the corner, I heard her calling for me, "Megan? Megan? My daughter is here, she will know." That day, her body had filled up with fluid again. It was filling up with fluid because the ovarian cancer she had beat once before, came back full force and planted itself on her liver. The hospital staff was adjusting her onto the cart when I arrived, "Yes mom, I am here," I responded, out of breath because I was in a rush to be by her side. "Date of birth?" The ER worker asked me as they assisted her onto the cart. "12/27/66" I replied, proud of myself for remembering her birthday.

We made it to a room and eventually a young resident came in to do his assessment on her. Palpating her swollen belly, he explained to me that fluid was building up in her stomach because her liver was not functioning properly. As he asked mom questions, I sat in the corner and I can still feel the knot I had in my throat as I realized how fast her health was spiraling out of our control. Reality seemed to be far away in my life up until that moment when I realized she really was sick this time. It was not a dream. As I think back to that moment, I can picture myself asking to be excused to the bathroom because I didn't want mom to see me cry. I felt like I needed to be strong for her. But as always, she noticed me get up and said, "Megan, don't cry," in her sweet soothing voice. "

My daughter is a nurse you know," I remember her telling the resident, smiling proudly. I recall being able to tell what she was trying to do. Even in the midst of being sick, mom was trying to play matchmaker. Back then, she hated my current boyfriend and told me over and over I deserved better. But I was not interested in the cute doctor or her attempts at playing matchmaker. I was interested in her health and all I wanted was for her to get better. I was beginning to feel hopeless as her sickness worsened.

My mind was going crazy with thoughts such as "Where do we go from here? Where are you God? Why is this happening to my family!?"

The next few weeks after that emergency room visit seemed to fly by. Eventually, mom's stomach began to swell again and she needed another procedure. I remember getting in the car with mom and dad that day as dad quickly and anxiously drove to the hospital. The doctor had agreed to do another procedure in an attempt to cause her liver to filter properly. As I sat in the waiting room, terrified, I wrote this as a Facebook post:

December 2013:

"I cannot explain to you how hard it is to watch a love one battle cancer. I can sit here and tell you about my dad breaking down crying at the kitchen table or describe to you the look on my brother and sisters face when they see how much weight she has lost. I can try and describe to you how scared we all are to lose her. Or tell you about the constant knot in my throat or the tears running down my face as I write this. I can tell you what it feels like to hold your mom when she has lost 30 lbs and she's crying because she is so scared or how she squeezed my hand before her procedure and said "see how strong I am!" I can sit here and tell you how strong she is and how big of a role model and inspiration she is. But the thing is,

I shouldn't be telling you any of this because she doesn't want anyone to know. It is so hard to respond to people with a forced smile when they ask how she is or respond with "You know her, she's just busy, always on the go." But that's not the truth. She knows how busy everyone is and doesn't want to ruin anyone's Christmas. But guess what? There is no good time for cancer and I can't hold it in anymore. So here I am sitting in the hospital with my dad, waiting and praying for her procedure to go well, trying to describe to you all of these emotions and feelings but no one understands until they have been through it. I am not telling you this for pity, I am hoping by reading this, maybe it will change someone's outlook on life. Maybe it will help someone let go of a grudge they have been holding against a loved one.

Maybe it will inspire someone to pick up the phone and call someone they haven't talked to in a while. I don't want pity, I want positivity. If you see any of my family members around, don't tell us you are sorry, tell me she will pull through, tell me you know how strong she is. Tell me about a love one you cherish. Tell me you are praying. And if you don't see me around, please take time to say a prayer for me and my family, give us strength to stay together and pull through this. All I have left to say if please hold on to your loved ones tight, and cherish each moment because life happens fast and tomorrow is never promised."

When I hit "post," we were flooded with comments and phone calls. I was comforted by the knowledge of people praying because in that moment, I was not sure that God was listening to my prayers. Mom eventually had a drain placed in the side of her stomach and was discharged from the hospital. We were sent home with a list of medications and instructions on how to drain her when she became uncomfortable. Unfortunately, the fluid kept filling her up and causing her to lose her appetite. Each time she ate, she would get sick. It was like a vicious cycle. Eventually on January 1st 2014 at 10am, she took her last breath. I remember writing in my journal:

"Mom had been up all night fish breathing and unable to talk. This type of breathing sounds like someone is drowning. Mom's body had filled up with fluid because her liver was failing. Mom loved foot rubs, so my brother Will was rubbing her feet. They were turning blue because they were starting to mottle. I will never forget Will's face when he was rubbing her feet and looked at me and said, "Megan, look." He looked terrified.

950am came and I had a feeling mom was getting ready to pass. I whispered to her "I will take care of them, it is okay mom, let go." My dad asked for a few moments alone with her. Then we came back in. She finally took her last breath, and my dad collapsed over her body in tears. "Jill, don't leave!"

After she had passed I went and got my brother and sister, they had gone to their rooms while Dad wanted his moment. I asked them if they wanted to see Mom for the last time, they came and saw her, we said a prayer over her body, and everything else seems like it was in fast forward."

After mom died, I took a long shower. I did not know what else to do. It was as if I felt like I could wash the day away. I felt completely lost as to what life would bring next. I felt completely numb. I believe this is part of the grieving process. They refer to it as shock. I remember sitting on the stairs with my cousin watching people enter and exit our house. I asked her what she thought would happen when all these people left and moved on with their lives. I asked her what we do when everyone else is moving forward and getting over the fact that she is gone when we are still grieving. I had no idea how to cope. I was not a true Christian at that time so when faced with tragedy, I did not know where to turn when my thirsty soul needed rejuvenated. Instead, I turned to people, alcohol, sex, TV shows, food, and drugs for satisfaction. My faith was based purely on how I was feeling at the moment. The Bible was not real to me. God was real to me, I just did not know how to find Him.

The reason I called this chapter "thirsty in the wilderness," is because when I think back to this moment in my life I think of Exodus 14. In this text, the Israelites trusted Moses enough to follow him out of Egypt into the Wilderness, but when they had reached a dead end path of either trusting him or being overcome with fear, they chose fear and cried out to the Lord:

"When Pharaoh drew near, the people of Israel lifted up their eyes, and behold, the Egyptians were marching after them, and they feared greatly. And the people of Israel cried out to the LORD." Exodus 14:10

When I read this, I picture myself in that scenario. Walking in the wilderness, attempting to put my faith into following Moses, attempting to trust that he is leading me to safety, but all I can see in front of me is the Red Sea, and all I can hear and see behind me are Pharaohs horses and chariots and his army drawing near. I can picture my knee's shaking and my doubt growing. Moses tells them to *"Fear not, stand firm, and see the salvation of the LORD, which he will work for you today. For the Egyptians whom you see today, you shall never see again*" (Exodus 14:13).

As much as I want to say that I would fear not, stand firm, and trust that God would pull through without any doubt plaguing my heart and causing me turn away from Him, the truth is, there is no way. I have a history of doubting God and being overcome with doubt, fear, and the desire to control a situation.

Before these words that Moses spoke, the people began to doubt God and say to Moses, *"Is it because there are no graves in Egypt that you have taken us away to die in the wilderness?"* (Exodus 14:11). Basically they are saying, "really God? You couldn't just kill us in Egypt? Why did you have to make us wander around and then bring us here to die?"

I love scripture because it is able to expose my weaknesses, like doubt and fear. Both have been very potent in my life. Just like the Israelites, when things were uncertain, like that day in the hospital with mom, I was guilty of losing faith, letting fear take over, doubting God, and trying to control the situation.

The unfortunate thing is that both I, and the children of Israel failed to realize the importance of Isaiah 55:8 *"For my thoughts are not your thoughts, neither are your ways my ways, declares the LORD."* The Lord is able to handle things in ways we would never dream of. In this text, He saved the people by parting the sea. I am sure the Israelites were not expecting God to save them by parting a sea, but our God works in amazing ways. This has certainly proven true in my life.

If you would have told me four years ago I would be writing this book, speaking at ladies days, married to an evangelist, dropping out of the military to be a missionary, pursuing a nurse practitioning degree to use in the mission field, leaning on God with my cancer, I would have told you, you were insane. Back then, I was on the path of spiritual dehydration, lost in my own wilderness, and Jesus was the last person on my mind.

Up until four years ago, being lost in the wilderness didn't seem to bad. I worked hard, and I most certainly played hard. I thought I was a decent person because I never went to jail or killed anyone. I believed that a hard day at work, deserved a glass of wine or night out with friends drinking at a bar. I thought church was just some building full of hypocrites that you were forced to visit on Sundays and Wednesdays because your parents were forced to when they were children. In my mind, nothing bad could ever happen to me because bad things only happen to strangers. I never questioned why I was on earth or even considered the possibility that I was not living the way I should. I played the victim every chance I could.

My faith was not built on a firm foundation, it was built on what I was feeling at the moment. Which explains the fact that I spiraled out of control when mom died. I had nothing to hold on to when things were uncertain. Long story short, a couple of months later after her death, I woke up in the hospital after three days spent there.

I cannot help but smile as I think back to the moment I woke up and as the night shift nurse was leaving, she handed me a Bible reading plan. Apparently, in my confusion during the night, I had asked her for one. I had been admitted to the hospital due to delirium from drug use and alcohol. I do not think going into detail is needed, but just know, I was in a very dark thirsty place. But the beautiful truth is that God was there with me. He was there with me through my Grandparents, aunts, uncles, and Dad who remained by my side, praying for me, until I came out of the confusion. He was also there for me through that nurse who provided that reading plan.

When I was discharged from the hospital I decided I was

going to spend a few months trying to find myself. I changed my phone number and stayed off social media for three months. I wanted to eliminate any type of influence in my life except for family. I questioned everything. I needed to discover who God was, and why I felt so distant from Him. During this time I prayed for guidance, asked for wisdom from people I knew were seasoned in the scriptures and never stopped asking questions. I prayed hard for a solution because if we are being honest here, I felt pretty empty and at a loss of where to begin.

One day while unpacking a box in our new home (we had moved out of the house mom died in, and into a new one) and I came across a book called *Muscle and a Shovel.* My aunt Tamera was staying with us to help us unpack and I asked her what it was. She said, "Oh it is a really good book I mailed your mom; you should check it out!" Once I started reading, I could not stop. This book changed my life and I am confident it will change yours. It pointed me to the Bible and broke it down so that I was able to look at it myself and not be so intimidated by it.

To be honest, when I realized I needed God, the Bible was the last place I thought to look. I was not even sure how to pray or if He even existed or why we were created. I used to think the Bible was just something that was supposed to sit on my bookshelf until Sunday came. I thought it was too complicated to understand. I remember reading it once and there were so many *"thee's* and *thou's,"* that it caused me to lose interest. But then I dug deeper. I prayed for guidance and each day I was pointed in the right direction. Scripture says: *"Ask, and it will be given to you; seek, and you will find; knock, and it will be opened to you"* (Matthew 7:7) and I have most certainly found this to be true.

The best lesson *Muscle and a Shovel* taught me was the realization that in order to find God, I had to blow off the dust from my Bible and start developing a relationship with Him. Once I realized I could understand His word, I could not stop reading it. Something I discovered that has benefited me greatly is that you do not have to be a Bible scholar to start studying the Bible. In addition, it is so full of information that is important to our lives today. It is not just some old fashioned book that judgmental people quote from as I once thought.

In the next few pages of this book, I want to spend time going through a review of the Bible because I do not know where you are in your Christian walk and I think it is important for you to be able to look at the Bible for yourself. I wish someone had done this for me, so I am doing it for you:

1 Peter 3:15 tells us: *"but in your hearts honor Christ the Lord as holy, always being prepared to make a defense to anyone who asks you for a reason for the hope that is in you; yet do it with gentleness and respect."* Something amazing happens when you are able to backup your beliefs with the Word of God and learn how to defend its inspiration. My goal in this section is to help you realize this and then confidently be able to be defend it. I remember the day I discovered that the Bible is truly inspired and it all started to make sense. It was as if a light bulb went off in my head. I hope this section of the book makes the Bible come to life for you as it did for me.

In 2 Timothy 3:16-17 we are told *"All Scripture is God-breathed and is useful for teaching, rebuking, correcting and training in righteousness, so that the servant of God may be thoroughly equipped for every good work.*" God literally breathed out His word through inspired men who wrote the words out for Him. The Bible was written in *Greek, Aramaic,* and *Hebrew.* Looking at the original language allows us to see detail and depth of meaning behind a word and eliminate confusion. Confusion happens when we do not check the original language for our meaning as it was intended and instead decide we will define what it means.

For example, the *Greek* word for baptism is *baptizo* which means fully immerse (biblestudytools.com). What happens today, is that certain translators are not properly translating. They failed to look at what the word meant in the original language, in the original time it was written. This has sadly resulted in various translations for baptism such as sprinkling, pouring, dipping.

Poor translation has resulted in thousands of denominations and various meanings derived from the Bible. Our God is an awesome God and He is not a God of confusion. One of my favorite pieces of knowledge I have gained is that when I am confused about a word, often times I am able to look up the root word and look at the whole context of what the passage is intending to say and the message is often clear.

• If you have a Bible near you, I want you to open it. Looking at the index helps locate the 66 books in the Bible. I used to be really intimidated because it seemed impossible to understand. I remember when I first started actually being *mentally* present in Bible class. The teacher would tell us to turn to a certain passage, and I felt so lost as everyone else was quickly turning to the correct page. I was embarrassed to look at the index. But I stopped comparing my day one in Christianity to their day fifty and started looking at the index to find the page number until I learned where each book was.

There are over forty different inspired writers who wrote these 66 books over a span of 1600 years with one common theme: a coming Savior. The Bible is divided in two sections: the Old and New Testament. The word "testament" means a covenant or agreement (Apologetics Press, 2001). The first book of the Bible is named Genesis which means beginning and this is where we learn about the beginning of the universe and everything in it. If you are anything like me, you have read the beginning section of the Bible until you got to the genealogies and then lost interest and put the book down. It gets better I promise!

Genesis includes the fall of man. God created the first man and placed him in a beautiful garden and saw that it was not good for him to be alone, so he created a helper suitable for him (a woman).

Later we read that Satan tempted the woman. God told them that they could have any type of food in the garden except the forbidden fruit. Unfortunately, the woman used her free will to disobey God, and this is when sin entered the world. This is also when they became separated from God. God is a just God, so when they disobeyed Him, He punished them and banished them.

After this, eventually people started becoming so evil that scripture says God regretted ever creating them (Genesis 6:5). God was so angry at man's sinful nature that He sent a flood to cover the entire earth. Only one man named Noah, his wife, three sons, and their wives were saved in the flood along with a certain number of animals.

After the flood, humans began to multiply on earth again and started sinning by worshiping many different gods. As we continue to read through Genesis we see that God chooses a man named Abraham to become the father of a nation that God set aside to be His chosen people. This takes awhile but we read that God does this by blessing Abraham with a child named Isaac who has a son named Jacob whose name is eventually changed to Israel (this is the section I was once guilty of skimming through). Twelve sons are eventually born to Jacob and they become the leaders of what came to be known as the twelve tribes of Israel.

After awhile, Jacob and his sons traveled to the land of Egypt where they became slaves. Even though they were slaves, God eventually redeemed them through a man named Moses. Moses and his brother Aaron were sent on a mission to free the Israelites. After escaping Egypt, God gives them a special law that separated them from all the other nations around them.

We can read more about this in the first five books of the Old Testament. A name that is used to define these first five books is the *Pentateuch* which means (five books). These books are Genesis, Exodus, Leviticus, Numbers, and Deuteronomy. This is where we read about God giving the Old Law to Moses to present to the Jews, Abraham becoming the father of the Jewish nation, the Jews becoming the chosen people of God, and the 12 tribes of Israel. Although there were many tedious laws that the Jews were told to follow, the Ten Commandments represented the major rules they were to live by.

As we read through the Old Testament we learn of the history of the Hebrews including the fact that they wanted to be like the nations around them, so they begged God for a king. God wanted to be their only King and he warned them of the bad things that would happen with a human king, but He allows them to go through with it. Unfortunately when this happens they were led in the wrong direction spiritually.

Once again they turned away from God and turned toward worshiping strange idols. The books 1&2 Samuel, 1&2 Kings, 1&2 Chronicles are filled with this information. God, being as patient as He is, sent prophets to the Jews to strongly influence them to come back to their creator but like many of us today, they were stubborn and refused to listen. The books Isaiah through Malachi will take us through their rebellion and failure to listen to the prophets.

The Jews failed to be obedient to the Old Law, they misused it or frankly ignored it so God promised that He would send another prophet. In Deuteronomy 18:15 we read that Moses said: *"The Lord your God will raise up for you a Prophet like me from your midst, from your brethren. Him you shall hear"* This new Prophet would arrive with a new law: *"Behold, the days are coming, says the Lord, when I will make a new covenant with the house of Israel and with the house of Judah"* (Jeremiah 31:31).

The Jews anxiously awaited the arrival of a Messiah who was said to bring salvation and a new covenant. The prophet Isaiah wrote that He would be *"despised and rejected by men, a man of sorrows, and acquainted with grief"*(Isaiah 53:3). He would be a Savior that would be put to death for the sins of His people in order to fulfill Gods demands of justice (Isaiah 53:5). This Messiah would establish a new law that would allow people from anywhere, not just the Jews, to be His chosen people. Which leads us to the New Testament.

In the New Testament we see 27 books consisting of Matthew through Revelation. These books are divided into four sections:

The Gospel Accounts: The term "gospel" refers to "good

news." The first four books are Matthew, Mark, Luke, and John. These are known as the gospel accounts because they reveal the story of our redeeming Savior: Jesus and His life, death, and resurrection.

History: This consists of Acts which is the "acts" of the apostles, the beginning of the church, and its early history. After Jesus went into Heaven, His followers began traveling the world to spread His gospel.

Epistles: this is another word for letter. As the apostles taught the gospel around the world, many churches were started in different cities. The apostles needed a way to explain to these churches the proper way to worship and how to live. So they wrote them letters. Sometimes the letters are written to an individual such as 1 and 2 Timothy, which were written by Paul to Timothy. These Epistles were written to Christians who needed encouragement, answers to questions, spiritual instruction, and sometimes even discipline. Paul wrote many of the letters in the New Testament. Sometimes he even wrote from prison!

Prophecy: This is the book of Revelation. It is called a prophetic book because it told the people in the first century what was going to happen to them in the future. If you decide to read through the book of Revelation, keep in mind that it uses lots of symbolic language which comes from the books of Daniel and Ezekiel because the Jews would understand and their enemies would not.

The New Testament was not written right after the Old.

God waits about 350 years after the last book in the Old Testament was written. Although written so much later, it picks up right where the Old Testament left off. All of the prophets had been teaching about the coming Messiah who would save the world from its sin and create a spiritual kingdom. The entire Jewish nation was waiting on this Messiah. As we read through the four gospel accounts we read the story of Jesus, His teachings, and His miracles which prove that He was the predicted Messiah.

Sadly, the Jews did not accept Jesus as their savior, and He is crucified. If the Bible stopped here, it would have been depressing. But something amazing happens. Jesus is resurrected and paves the way for us to be reunited with God.

The rest of the New Testament presents the new covenant that Jesus established. This new covenant meant that people no longer had to make animal sacrifices or needed a priest to help them repent from their sins. Jesus' own death on the cross would be the only sacrifice that could forgive sins. When Jesus was nailed to the cross scripture says He nailed the Old law to the cross with Him (Colossians 2:14).

The Old Testament is not just filled with boring books of the Old Law. It is filled with stories of God's people turning away from Him, His wrath and punishment because of it, and eventually Him redeeming the ones who obeyed Him. Many of these stories are so encouraging, but also very frightening. In Romans 15:4 we are told: *"For whatever was written in former days was written for our instruction, that through endurance and through the encouragement of the Scriptures we might have hope."*

Maybe you are reading this and saying, "what does this have to do with me?" Or maybe you skipped the pages where

I overviewed the Bible. If you did, I would highly encourage you to go back and read. I want us to begin with a solid foundation. I want you to know that I believe that understanding the Bible has everything to do with you. Since you are reading this book, chances are you are struggling with something. Whether it be struggling to find your identity, or purpose, or feeling lost and unsure. I do not have the answers and I will not pretend to. I will however, point you to someone who does. That is what I am trying to accomplish here. I want to point you to the scriptures because it is there I found the answers to my search for an identity, purpose, attention, acceptance, comfort, and love.

So go back and review. Go back and find yourself in Exodus 14. What would have been your response to Moses leading you out of Egypt? Would you have been fearful? Or would you have trusted that the Lord was leading you to a better place?

Thirst Quenching Questions

What would your response be if Pharoah was chasing you and the Red Sea was in front of you? Would you trust God?

Read Exodus 14:13; what does it mean to stand firm?

How firm are you in your beliefs?

Read Ephesians 6:10-19; what are some ways to stand firm from these scriptures?

Read Galatians 5:1; what has Christ set us free from?

What is sin?

Read Romans 3:23 and write it here

According to this have you sinned?

Read Romans 6:23; what is the outcome of sin?

Read Romans 5:12 and write it here:

According to this verse, how did death enter the world?

Read Ephesians 2: 1-5 and write it here:

Ephesians 2:3 refers to passions of the flesh. Write out the passions of the flesh according to Galatians 5:19:

Have the fruits of the flesh in Gal 5:19 caused any of the "thirsts" in your life?

Read Ephesians 5:8-9 and compare it to Galatians 5:20- 24. Write about being in the light vs darkness and the fruit from each.

List the fruits of the spirit in Galatians 5:22, how pursuing these be a solution to our thirsts?

Read Romans 6:15-16; what are the two options we have to be a slave to?

Which one are you currently a slave to?

Read Hebrews 11:1-29

From this passage, is faith based on an action, or just emotion?

Compare this with your faith:

Week Three: Thirsty for an Identity

"Then Jesus told his disciples, If anyone would come after me, let him deny himself and take up his cross and follow me." Matthew 16:24

Placing yourself in the shoes of the children of Israel while Moses is leading them out of bondage should have caused you to either be filled with faith or fear. If you found yourself with fear, don't worry, I was once there, but I found a solution to replacing fear with faith. My solution involves discovering our true identities.

After months of isolating myself and digging deep into the scriptures, I decided to start hanging out with old friends again. I had stopped drinking alcohol, but I thought I could still go out to the places my friends wanted to go. One night in particular, I was at a country bar and there was loud music playing. My friends were talking to other people and I was just standing there feeling out of place. A man at the bar looked at me and said "Hey! Let me buy you a drink!" I smiled and said "No thank you I don't drink." He asked in a harsh, judgmental tone, "Then, why are you here?" I remember thinking to myself, "good question, why am I here?" I felt totally out of place. I never went back to a bar after that. I felt confident my identity was no longer found in friends and drinking.

I was thirsty for a new identity. Once I stopped going out and drinking, people I thought were my friends stopped calling to hang out. It seemed when alcohol was not involved, we had nothing left in common. I felt lonely, but determined to continue on this path.

Sunday's and Wednesday's became my favorite days because I had finally decided to be *mentally* present at worship and I began learning so much. I introduced myself to fellow members that I should have known by then but did not know because in the past, I always came to worship late and always rushed out to get to somewhere else I had to be. I was only there to avoid a lecture from my parents.

One Sunday, the sermon was about anxiety. Our minister was preaching from Matthew 6:25-34. These verses discuss the importance of letting God worry about your problem's. One verse he started with was *"But seek first the kingdom of God and his righteousness, and all these things will be added to you"* Matthew 6:33. I sat there wondering how to seek the kingdom of God.

He continued and stated that worry shows a lack of faith and asked the congregation *"do we really believe in the promises of God; if we did, why would we be anxious?"* Questions began to flood my mind. Did I truly believe in the promises of God? What are the promises of God? How do I seek the kingdom of heaven? What is faith?

As I wrestled with these questions, one day I found mom's old Bible and in it, the verse Matthew 7:21-23 was highlighted which says " *"Not everyone who says to me, 'Lord, Lord,' will enter the kingdom of heaven, but the one who does the will of my Father who is in heaven. On that day many will say to me, 'Lord, Lord, did we not prophesy in your name, and cast out demons in your name, and do many mighty works in your name?' And then will I declare to them, 'I never knew you; depart from me, you workers of lawlessness."* When I read this, I became anxious. I had attended church for sixteen years and still did not know why I was truly there or whether I was doing the will of God.

I devoted time to figuring out these questions. I began to notice that when it came to a discussion about faith, people in our congregation often quoted, *"So faith comes from hearing, and hearing by the word of God"* Romans 10:17. I realized my faith was not built on the word of God, it was built on how I felt in my heart at the moment. Following my heart became hard when I came across Jeremiah 17:9 which states, *"The heart is deceitful above all things, and desperately sick; who can understand it?"* This verse caused me to wonder why I was following my heart and not the word of God. So I went to the word of God to see what it had to say. These are my findings:

Ephesians 2:8 tells us *"For by grace you have been saved through faith. And this is not your own doing; it is the gift of God,"* (Ephesians 2:8).

'I wanted to know what it meant to be saved by faith and what that had to do with grace. When I started comparing these verses with examples of grace and faith in other places in scripture, I realized that my view on these concepts was inconsistent. I thought that having faith meant just believing. But when I opened to the book of James, I discovered something different. James 2:14-17 says, *"What good is it, my brothers, if someone says he has faith but does not have works? Can that faith save him? If a brother or sister is poorly clothed and lacking in daily food, and one of you says to them, "Go in peace, be warmed and filled," without giving them the things needed for the body, what good is that? So also faith by itself, if it does not have works, is dead."* It was clear that having faith required more than just believing. So I began to look for examples of this.

I had remembered hearing lots of people in my congregation talk about the book of Hebrews and how it often describes those who had faith. So I began there. Hebrews 11:7 states, *"By faith Noah, being warned by God concerning events as yet unseen, in reverent fear constructed an ark for the saving of his household. By this he condemned the world and became an heir of the righteousness that comes by faith.* Growing up, I had always heard the story of Noah, but I never paid attention to the details, so I re-read his story and discovered something interesting.

Genesis 6:8 states that Noah found grace in the eyes of the Lord. However, we see in Hebrews 11:7 it says, "*By faith Noah, being warned by God concerning events as yet unseen, in rev-*

erent fear constructed an ark for the saving of his household." Noah found grace, but he did it by preaching the truth and being obedient. God gave grace to Noah. This grace was not something Noah could have done for himself; but it still required Noah to have faith and accept it by being obedient and building the ark.

Another example on obedience is Naaman. In 2 Kings 5, we discover he was the commander of the army for the king of Syria. He was a great and honorable man in the eyes of his master because by him the Lord had given victory to Syria and was also a mighty man of valor. But Naaman had a problem; he was a leper. In one of the their raids, the Syrians had carried a young captive girl from the land of Israel, and she worked in the service of Naaman's wife. The young girl told Naaman's wife *"If only my master were with the prophet who is in Samaria! For he would heal him of his leprosy."* Naaman's wife must have told him about the potential solution to his problem because in the next verse we read that Naaman went to his master and told him what the girl had said.

The prophet whom the girl was referring to is the great Elisha from Gilgal. We read that he did amazing works in the previous chapter of 2 Kings. 2 Kings 5:10 tells us that Elisha tells Naaman to *"Go and wash in the Jordan seven times, and your flesh shall be restored to you and you shall be clean."*

You would think that Naaman would be really excited that he has a chance to be healed from leprosy, but what was his response? He becomes angry and proclaims his own desire of how he wants to be healed.

Scripture says *"But Naaman became furious and went away and said, "Indeed I said to myself, He will surely come out to me and stand and call on the name of the Lord his God and wave his hand over the place and heal the leprosy."*

And then he proceeds to say,

"Are not the Abanah and the Pharpar, the rivers of Damascus, better than all the waters of Israel? Could I not wash in them and be clean?"

And finally, "*he turned and went away in a rage.*" He eventually decided to listen and was cleansed of his leprosy by following specific instructions.

Naaman's solution did not involve him being sincere or believing with all of his heart that he would be cleansed his way. It involved humbling himself, being obedient to God's direction, and being cleansed in water. We see this in the next verse, *"So he went down and dipped himself seven times in the Jordan, according to the word of the man of God, and his flesh was restored like the flesh of a little child, and he was clean."* 2 Kings 5:14. He was unable to *believe* himself healed of leprosy.

It became clear in the Bible that God saves us by grace by providing us a way to escape death through His Son. However, according to scripture, it requires more than just believing. From scripture we see that we have to take action and be obedient to God's word. Someone may bring up the fact that both of those examples are in the Old Testament, but remember Paul?

In Acts 9 we read about Paul. Before he became a worker for Christ, He was killing Christians because he sincerely believed he was doing the right thing. But the Lord confronted Paul and struck him with blindness. Paul tried for three days to fast, and that did not work. It took more. The fact that Paul only believed did not save him, he had to be obedient to God's direction through Ananias. In verse 18 we read, *"So Ananias departed and entered the house. And laying his hands on him he said, "Brother Saul, the Lord Jesus who appeared to you on the road by which you came has sent me so that you may regain your sight and be filled with the Holy Spirit." And immediately something like scales fell from his eyes, and he regained his sight." Then he rose and was baptized."*

Paul was not saved until he arose and was baptized. Like Paul, Noah, Naaman, and so many others, our faith cannot just be based on how we feel. We have to have faith that takes action.

My desire is not to convince you to believe what I believe,it is to gently, and respectfully, point you to scripture and encourage you to have a firm defense for your beliefs, aside from saying *"I believe in my heart..."*

Many of us are okay with the fact that we are sinners because we acknowledge the fact that Jesus died for our sins. It is comfortable to talk about the love of God, but what about the justice of God? If we leave out the fact that God is just, we tend to use circular reasoning for why God sent His son to die for us (Mosher, 2015). So in a conversation with someone, it often looks like this, *"God loves you, so He sent His son to die for you. Why? Because He loves you; therefore He sent His son."* This does not really make since, does it?

If we go back to the garden and remember what God told Adam and Eve would happen to them if they disobeyed Him, we see that He told them they would die. He was talking about both physical and spiritual death. God is honest and fair, so He had to punish them, just like He said He would. This punishment still exists today. Death spread to us all, we see this in Romans 5:12 *"Therefore, just as sin came into the world through one man, and death through sin, and so death spread to all men because all sinned."*

In the past, when it came to the sin in my life, I often found myself trying to justify my sin by saying "I have never killed anyone, so my sin cannot be that bad." But in the garden, Adam and Eve did not kill anyone either, their sin was that they simply disobeyed God. Romans 3:23 tells us *"for all have sinned and fall short of the glory of God."* We are also told in Romans 6:23 *"the wages of sin is death."* God could have just left us in this state, but He is a loving God and has provided us another chance to be with Him again. This is where Jesus comes in. *"For God so loved the world, that he gave his only Son, that whoever believes in him should not perish but have eternal life. For God did not send his Son into the world to condemn the world, but in order that the world might be saved through him"* John 3:16-17.

When I read this, I had a moment of clarity. God sent His Son so that we could have faith by choosing to believe in Him and choose to be saved from death through Him. We have free will to choose to believe or choose to turn our backs on Him. He is not going to force anyone to love and obey Him. It is up to us to be saved from God's wrath through Jesus. I love how it is written in Romans 5:8-11 *"but God shows his love for us in that while we were still sinners, Christ died for us. Since, therefore, we have now been justified by his blood, much more shall we be saved by him from the wrath of God. For if while we were enemies we were reconciled to God by the death of his Son, much more, now that we are reconciled, shall we be saved by his life. More than that, we also rejoice in God through our Lord Jesus Christ, through whom we have now received reconciliation."*

I had always heard our congregation talk about the "gospel" but never fully understood it until I started to pay more attention. This is what I found:

The word *gospel* means good news. The good news is that when Adam and Even failed to obey God in the beginning of time, causing death to enter the world and us to be separated from Him, God gave us another chance. Instead of letting us remain in that state, He had a plan set in motion to save us. This plan is seen throughout the whole Old Testament. After the first sin, there were over 300 prophecies about a coming Savior (Thompson, 2000). In the New Testament we read that Jesus fulfilled the Old Testament scriptures by being nailed to the cross. We see this in

1 Corinthians 15:3-4
"For I delivered to you as of first importance what I also received: that Christ died for our sins in accordance with the Scriptures, that he was buried, that he was raised on the third day in accordance with the Scriptures..."

He conquered death. He became sin for us. His obedience to the cross allows us to have access to God. The good news is that we can have a true identity in Christ! The key word here is "in." It is only when we get INTO Christ that we are able to be added to the Lord's church and obtain our new identity. But how?

If we turn in our Bibles to Galatians 3:27 we read, *"For as many of you as were baptized into Christ have put on Christ."* This shows that baptism puts us into Christ. But does it save us? Let's look at 1 Peter 3:21. This tells us *"Baptism, which corresponds to this, now saves you, not as a removal of dirt from the body but as an appeal to God for a good conscience, through the resurrection of Jesus Christ,."*

So baptism puts us into Christ and saves us. But why? I think the answer is clear when we read Romans 6:1-3 *"What shall we say then? Are we to continue in sin that grace may abound? By no means! How can we who died to sin still live in it? Do you not know that all of us who have been baptized into Christ Jesus were baptized into his death? We were buried therefore with him by baptism into death, in order that, just as Christ was raised from the dead by the glory of the Father, we too might walk in newness of life."*

When we are baptized, our sins are washed away, we are obedient to God, and we come up out of the water a new creature in Christ. When we are immersed into the watery grave of baptism, we die to our old identity; when we come up out of the water, we put on our new identities in Christ Jesus. Just like Noah, Naaman, and Paul, our faith becomes more than just a feeling or words.

Let's look at some examples of following the gospel in the New Testament just to be sure: I recommend using the KJV, NKJV, or ESV versions of the Bible.

Phillip and the Eunuch: Acts 8:26-40. What happened? Summarize it here:

Paul: Acts 9: What happened? Summarize it here:

The Philippian Jailer: Acts 16:25-33. What happened? Summarize it here:

Cornelius and His household: Acts 10. Summarize it here:

What do each of these have in common? They had faith by hearing the word of God, believed in Jesus, repented (which means to turn away), confessed their sin, were immersed in water and added to the Lord's church.

Growing up, when it came to attending different churches, I always heard my friends say *"choose whatever one feels like home."* I used to think nothing of this, but now I cringe which I hear this. I cringe because church is not something you "go" to, it is something you are. When I open my Bible and read in the New Testament, I read about only one church, but when I look around me, I see thousands (WVBS, 2012).There are over 38,000 different churches (WVBS, 2012). Something must have gone wrong.

In Matthew 16:18 Jesus says *"And I tell you, you are Peter, and on this rock I will build my church, and the gates of hell shall not prevail against it."* While reading this I realized that Jesus did not say He would build multiple churches, He said I will build

MY church. As I told you before, during this journey I learned that it is important to look back at the original meaning of a word in scripture so that it is what I did in this case. I asked myself, "what does church mean in Greek?" It turns out the Greek term for church is *ekklesia* (Jackson, 2018). It is applied in these ways:

•It represents the body of Christ worldwide, over which Christ functions as head (Mt. 16:18; Eph. 1:22; 1 Tim. 3:15).

•It can refer to God's people in a given region (Acts 9:31, ASV, ESV).

•Frequently, it is depicted as a local congregation of Christians (1 Cor. 1:2; Rev. 1:11).

•It could also signify a group of the Lord's people assembled for worship (1 Cor. 14:34-35).

•There is only one (Ephesians 4:4).

/The word *ekklesia* is a compound of two segments: *ek*, a preposition meaning *"out of,"* and a verb, *kaleo*, signifying *"to call"* — hence, *"to call out,"* (Jackson, 2018).

In Acts 2, Jesus established His church through Peter on the day of Pentecost. Scripture says:

"But Peter, standing with the eleven, lifted up his voice and addressed them: "Men of Judea and all who dwell in Jerusalem, let this be known to you, and give ear to my words. For these people are not drunk, as you suppose, since it is only the third hour of the day. But this is what was uttered through the prophet Joel:
"'And in the last days it shall be, God declares,
that I will pour out my Spirit on all flesh,
and your sons and your daughters shall prophesy,
and your young men shall see visions,
and your old men shall dream dreams;
even on my male servants and female servants
in those days I will pour out my Spirit, and they shall prophesy.

And I will show wonders in the heavens above
and signs on the earth below,
blood, and fire, and vapor of smoke;
the sun shall be turned to darkness
and the moon to blood,
before the day of the Lord comes, the great and magnificent day.
And it shall come to pass that everyone who calls upon the name of the Lord shall be saved.'

"Men of Israel, hear these words: Jesus of Nazareth, a man attested to you by God with mighty works and wonders and signs that God did through him in your midst, as you yourselves know— this Jesus, delivered up according to the definite plan and foreknowledge of God, you crucified and killed by the hands of lawless men. God raised him up, loosing the pangs of death, because it was not possible for him to be held by it. For David says concerning him,

"'I saw the Lord always before me,
for he is at my right hand that I may not be shaken;
therefore my heart was glad, and my tongue rejoiced;
my flesh also will dwell in hope.
For you will not abandon my soul to Hades,
or let your Holy One see corruption.
You have made known to me the paths of life;
you will make me full of gladness with your presence.'

"Brothers, I may say to you with confidence about the patriarch David that he both died and was buried, and his tomb is with us to this day. Being therefore a prophet, and knowing that God had sworn with an oath to him that he would set one of his descendants on his throne, he foresaw and spoke about the resur-

rection of the Christ, that he was not abandoned to Hades, nor did his flesh see corruption. This Jesus God raised up, and of that we all are witnesses. Being therefore exalted at the right hand of God, and having received from the Father the promise of the Holy Spirit, he has poured out this that you yourselves are seeing and hearing. For David did not ascend into the heavens, but he himself says,

"'The Lord said to my Lord,

"Sit at my right hand,

until I make your enemies your footstool."'

Let all the house of Israel therefore know for certain that God has made him both Lord and Christ, this Jesus whom you crucified."

Now when they heard this they were cut to the heart, and said to Peter and the rest of the apostles, "Brothers, what shall we do?" And Peter said to them, "Repent and be baptized every one of you in the name of Jesus Christ for the forgiveness of your sins, and you will receive the gift of the Holy Spirit."

On this day, 3000 people were added to the Lord's church. Back then, the way to become a part of this church did not require taking a test, paying a bunch of money, asking Jesus into your heart, or sacrificing your first born. It required faith AND obedience.

Check out verse 37-38 again

"Now when they heard this they were cut to the heart, and said to Peter and the rest of the apostles, "Brothers, what shall we do?" And Peter said to them, "Repent and be baptized every one of you in the name of Jesus Christ for the forgiveness of your sins, and you will receive the gift of the Holy Spirit."

It says, *repent* and be *baptized* for the forgiveness of sins. All along I thought the church was some building you visit on Christmas and Easter, but it turns out, the church is much more than that.

After months of studying and paying attention at worship, I realized I was living my life completely wrong. I was baptized and when I came up out of that water, I was a completely new creature (2 Corinthians 5:17). I found my true identity. You see, the first time I was baptized I did it for all of the wrong reasons. It was just a show for my friends and family. I was not ready to live for God. I was not ready to commit to a Christian life and work in the Lord's church. I gave Him my left overs and expected to feel close to Him. I had one foot in the world and tried to put one foot in the church. But according to God's word, it does not work like that and Jesus could not fulfill my life's thirst if I continued living that way. I had to be all in or all out. Jesus tells us this in 1 John 1:6 *"if we say we have fellowship with him while we walk in darkness, we lie and do not practice the truth."*

I decided to be all in. Clarity in regards to my true identity was found the day I realized how badly I need Christ and His church. Once I discovered the grace He offers and the solution He provides to escape my worldly identity as a sinner, I was fulfilled and my fear was replaced with faith.

If we accept this as our new identity, it involves constantly humbling ourselves and acknowledging the sovereignty of God. It involves realizing that God is omniscient, meaning He knows all things about our past, present, and future, so when we pray, He knows our every need. Prayer becomes comforting when we are able to realize that He is working all things together to bring about His will and that if we are seeking to accomplish His will, all things eventually work together for good (Romans 8:28). The most freeing way to live is to live our lives for His glory. It is an amazing and fulfilling feeling, but not everyone will accept it.

Thirst Quenching Questions

Reflect on your current identity; what types of qualities define you as a person?

Are the things you are finding your identity in leaving you feeling filled, or thirsty?

Read Galatians 2:20; what are your thoughts on this type of identity?

In today's society, we are encouraged to find ourselves, but what does Matthew 16:24 say?

In your life, do you currently deny yourself?

How can denying ourselves, help us find our true identities in Christ? Compare this with Matthew 16:25

In Solomon's writing, Ecclesiastes 2:1-11, he describes his worldly pursuits. What pursuits in this generation are the same as his?

Are any of these pursuits contributing to your life thirst?

Are these pursuits defining your identity?

What changes can you take in your Christian life to avoid finding your identity in worldly pursuits?

Read Matthew 4:19; what does it mean to follow Jesus?

Do you find it hard to obey this verse? What holds you back the most?

Compare what holds you back to Galatians 1:10:

Read Ephesians 2:10; from this verse, what were created for?

After all his worldly pursuits, what were Solomon's final thoughts from Ecclesiastes 12:13?

What does it mean to fear God?

Read John 15:14; how are we friends with Jesus?

Reflect on what you what you have learned this far:

Week Four: Thirsty for Bad Boys

"Do not be unequally yoked with unbelievers. For what partnership has righteousness with lawlessness? Or what fellowship has light with darkness?" 2 Corinthians 6:14

As a Christian woman, one of the best pieces of knowledge I have gained is that there is a difference between being alone and lonely. I would have never admitted it, because at the time, I always said "I am an independent woman!" But there was a time when I used to feel like I always needed to be in a relationship. I needed someone to turn to for help or comfort. Even though I found my new identity in Christ, I still struggled with being alone. As a result, I often settled for toxic relationships.

In 1 Kings we read of a man named Solomon. He was David's son and he excelled all the other kings of the earth in riches and wisdom (1 Kings 10:23). In the first 10 chapters of 1 Kings, Solomon is doing great things for the Lord. But then we get to chapter 11, and things take a turn. God had told Solomon to stay away from certain women because He knew they would turn Solomons heart after other gods (1 Kings 11:2). But Solomon did not listen to this advice. He chose the other women over God. Scripture says that he *"clung to these in love,"* (1 Kings 11:2). The result was not a pleasant one: *"For when Solomon was old his wives turned away his heart after other gods, and his heart was not wholly true to the Lord his God, as was the heart of David his father,"* (1 Kings 11:4). When I read this, I am annoyed with Solomon. I am annoyed because God had been there for Him the whole time, and what does he do? He chooses some random women over Him.

Prior to one of my doctor appointments, I was asked to write down everything I ate for two weeks. At my appointment, he did not even look at it. But being forced to write down things I ate, made me realize how poorly I was eating. There were a few food choices that I ate and I thought to myself "man I do not want to write this down; this is embarrassing, and so unhealthy for me," but I wrote it down. By writing it down, it was brought to it light, and I was able to learn healthy alternatives. I was held accountable. I think this applies to our Christian lives as well. By writing down what we struggle with, we hold ourselves accountable.

As much as I did not want to write about my past relationships, doing so helped me become accountable. I began to realize that I was a lot like Solomon. I chose relationships over God. I am a bit embarrassed to discuss this, but I want my poor choices to be brought to light so that we can learn "healthy alternatives."

A dive into the history of my relationships reveals that I often pursued relationships with people that drew me away from God. I often pursued people I thought I could fix or I felt needed my help. Pursuing a Christian was the last thing on my mind. Christians made me feel judged and vulnerable. People who I felt were broken like me, were easier to identify with. Mom used to tell me I needed to quit trying to fix people and work on myself first. I ignored her advice of course, because I was in my early twenties and knew everything (so I thought).

In the first few chapters of my life, we can read about bad boy number one. By "bad," I mean he didn't have a car, job, or phone. He was into partying, his motto was "who cares, you only live once." I was in love with this bad boy and in my eyes, he loved me. I saw hope in him. He was always the life of the party and a lot of girls wanted to be with him. I also thought by being with him I could help him become motivated about life, and want to be successful. I believed I could change him. After all, I heard once, "he will change when he finds the right woman."

Over time he made baby steps. He became a better person. I saw progress in him. Slowly, but surely he got a job, a car, and a phone. But then life happened and his party boy mentality got the best of him and he ended up with a DUI. Which meant no car, and no job... Back to square one.

In 2012, I had decided to go to nursing school. So mom and dad helped me pick an apartment near the school in Newark, Ohio. However, little did they know, I was housing this bad boy with me. Over time, he was back to no car, no job, no phone. But no worries, I told people: "Stop being so judgmental, people make mistakes, and he promised he's changing his ways, so I'll give him another chance."

Plus, I had all those things he was lacking. I could help him. I mean, I joined the military and worked as a waitress. I didn't care about paying all the bills. I didn't care that he left all the lights on, trashed my car, hardly picked up after himself. I didn't care that I worked two jobs while he sat at home on the couch, drank beer, and ran up my cable bill. After all, he loved me and supported me.

My parents weren't dumb, but they didn't know he stayed all the time. They didn't know he practically lived there. He would take me to work and use my car, and do who knows what with who knows who. But, I didn't care. I didn't mind paying bills. I've never been materialistic. Especially when I'm in "love." It was okay, he did the dishes, he cleaned, and he loved me. Plus all these other women wanted to be with him and he was mine! Right? Riiight...

I constantly told my mom she was wrong. He was not going to bring me down, I was going to bring him up. The more she told me to break up with him, the more I fought to stay with him. After all she didn't know him like I did, and I was determined to prove her wrong

I ignored the advice of other loved ones as well, "You just wait," I would say. He would change. He is a good person. I would tell my friends, "He says things will be different, and I believe him." The fact is, he never changed, and he grew *more* dependent.

Time went by and I started feeling trapped in my own apartment. I started feeling like I was raising a child. Our relationship became toxic. Even though I was in a relationship, I felt alone. I was working two jobs and trying to survive nursing school while he was asking me for money to buy beer. I would get out of the shower and he would be going through my phone. He even demanded my Facebook password. I gave in because I knew he had insecurities from his past relationships.

What I didn't know was this: When someone is so worried that you are cheating, and constantly needs to know your whereabouts, who you talk to, what you're doing, it's not only unhealthy, but it is 95% because THEY are the one cheating, and are terrified you are doing what they are.

Long story short, four years later, filled with lots of arguments, complicated trust issues between us, and other draining situations, he didn't change. Precious time was wasted trying to fix him and believing in someone who didn't believe in himself.

After many failed attempts and running back to him after I broke up with him, I finally grew enough courage to end things permanently. I remember going on a walk with mom and telling her the news, she was so happy, she almost did a cartwheel. I was glad to not fight with her anymore. She never once said, "I told you so." But she was completely right. Yes, he had issues. But, he was not the problem. I was. I needed to realize I couldn't fix someone. He needed to fix himself. He needed to believe in himself. He needed to want those things that I wanted for him. If he was going to change, it would be because HE wanted to.

Perhaps through the heartache, I planted a seed in his heart that would be watered by someone one day and hopefully God would give the increase. But it is he who needed to overcome his own sins, I was not the one who could do it.

I needed to work on myself. I needed to have more confidence, and to realize I deserved better. There are so many girls out there that remind me of myself, and I hope a few of you read this and escape while you can. It was extremely hard to end my relationship. Ask my best friend, and anyone that came to my birthday party that night. I cried all night like a baby, like my life was over. It took awhile to heal, but I did, and you will, too.

Some people are not so blessed to remove themselves from toxic relationships. They end up being blessed with a precious baby. The baby more than likely ends up with just a sperm donor because his father is still out trying to find himself.

I did not end up with a child from my former toxic relationship, but I have friends who did. Babies are a gift from God. Who knows what an amazing person that baby could turn out to be with a Godly mother! The goal of sharing this is that maybe someone will read this and realize they deserve better before they end up being a single mom. There is a reason God said to save sex for marriage, it is not just because He is strict. He loves us and He knows the pain that comes with giving yourself to someone who is not completely devoted to you in marriage.

If you are reading this and you are in a current relationship where you feel like you are trying to change the man please get out while you can. Let him find Jesus, himself, and then come find you when he's actually ready to be in a relationship.

Once I realized I did not need a man to complete me, I reflected on my past relationships and learned that I wanted an equal, a partner, a teammate. Not someone I needed to fix and drag along through life, hoping they become motivated. I wanted the type of love described in 1 Corinthians 13:4-7:

"Love is patient and kind; love does not envy or boast; it is not arrogant or rude. It does not insist on its own way; it is not irritable or resentful; it does not rejoice at wrongdoing, but rejoices with truth. Love bears all things, believes all things, hopes all things, endures all things."

This type of love is demonstrated with action. Not words.

Before I made the decision to be single and become the woman of God I needed to be, I made a commitment to find this type of love, so I started online dating. I attempted not settle for anything less that 1 Corinthians 13:4-7, but I had a bad habit of falling for the bad boys.

This second bad boy came into my life during the time my mom was passing away. He was not the type of bad I had experience with before. He had an awesome job and his own place. He would come over when I wanted to be with mom. One night, he even carried her up stairs when she was too weak to walk. He took off work to be by my side during her funeral. I was convinced I had found "the one." But there was just one problem. He had zero interest in waiting to have sex before marriage and zero interest in the church. In fact, he mocked it, and mocked me for attending.

After I was baptized, I had decided that summer I was done drinking, but told myself I could still hang out with people who did. I would even be willing to date someone who did. At first it was cute, and I could deal with it. But then I started to realize that he was more interested in drinking and having fun than he was pursuing the Christian life style with me.

One day, I was his designated driver and we were arguing about something in the car. I remember thinking to myself, "I will never let someone make me feel like this again; I can't be around this kind of lifestyle anymore." It was as if in that moment I had an awakening. I was finally strong enough to not settle. When we arrived at his apartment, we were in the middle of an intimate moment and I looked at him and said, "I can't do this, I feel like I am hurting God." He looked at me like I had lost my mind. But I knew I hadn't. You see, I had known my whole life that sex before marriage was wrong. However, until I started studying more, I did not realize how bad it actually is.

A few days before that moment, I had read 1 Corinthians 6:12-15 and realized that if I believed I was wearing Christ, and the Bible says to save sex for marriage, I was basically making Him participate in things that He did not want to. How was I any better than those people who nailed him to the cross?

I tried to express how I felt to bad boy numer two, but bad boy number two told me that he did not understand, and that I needed a new hobby instead of going to church all the time. He told me that I would never meet someone that had the same views, and I would end up settling for some lame Christian boy. This was tempting to believe, but God proved this wrong.

When bad boy number two and I ended things, I focused more on becoming a woman of God and less on finding a relationship. At first, it was scary. I was terrified of being alone because I had always been in a relationship since high school. But then I began to view being single as a gift instead of a burden and finally started to feel free.

During my time of being single, I lost thirty nine pounds because I stopped using food for comfort, started working out, and began developing healthy eating habits. I was also smoking at the time and realized I needed to quit. I remember being on the treadmill at the gym and watching a commercial talk about how CVS was no longer selling cigarettes because it goes against what they believe in. There I was, smoking while studying nursing, practically destroying my body. The day I quit, I dumped water into my pack of cigarettes and made a vow to God that I would never pick them up again. I have kept that vow four years later.

During my time of being single, I finally understood the difference between being alone and lonely and the positive aspect of solitude. I think Jesus even demonstrated this quality. In Matthew 14:23 we read: *"After He had sent the crowds away, He went up on the mountain by Himself to pray; and when it was evening, He was there alone."* Jesus knew the benefit of being alone in the presence of God. I never understood this until I forced myself to spend time alone studying God's word and praying.

I found my worth as a new creature in Christ instead of in another person. I cannot explain to you how empowering it felt to understand my worth and purpose and to develop a healthy life-style. When I began to date again, I was very picky. At first, I felt guilty, but then I realized, I was allowed to be picky. I was a child of God and I knew what I wanted. I invited each prospect to church. The ones that were willing, I devoted time to. The ones who were not, I let go. It may sound harsh, but I had new goals and standards, I stuck to them and was blessed with an amazing husband you will meet in a later chapter.

It is easy to fall for the lie that there are no good men left. Satan convinces us through this society that there are no godly men, so we often settle. But believe me when I tell you, they are out there and they are worth the wait!

You are also worth the wait. If you are settling because you are lonely, I completely understand, but we have to break this habit! No one will ever fix that loneliness inside of you except Christ. You are a beautiful child of God and He has high standards for the men we put in our lives. You are aloud to have high standards as well.

Thirst Quenching Questions

What is the difference between being alone and being lonely?

Analyze the things or people you turn to for comfort; are they healthy things? Are they spiritual things? If not, what are some alternatives?

Is your current relationship helping you draw closer to God, or turning your heart from Him?

Read 2 Corinthians 6:14, are you currently unequally yoked?

Read 1 Corinthians 6:12-15; who does vs 15 tell us we are members of?

If we are members of Christ, and we are having sex before marriage, how are we any different than the ones nailing Him to the cross?

Plug the name of the person you are dating in the place of "Love" in 1 Corinthians 13. Does he fit the description?

Plug your name into 1 Corinthians 13 in the place of "love." Do you fit the description?

What do you need to change about yourself to fit the description?

How can you use your singleness to bring God glory?

Week Five: Thirsty for Attention

"Even the very hairs on your head are numbered."
Matthew 10:30

Writing this book has proven to be a daunting task. It has required me to dig deep into my past to reveal the reasons for the constant thirsts in my life. One contributing factor that influenced the way I lived my life in the past, was the thirst for attention.

The type of attention I was thirsty for before I was devoted to living a Christ driven life was the kind you get from wearing daisy duke shorts and a tiny tank top to the county fair. This was not Godly attention. I found self-worth from random guys whistling and yelling cat calls as I walked by.

There was a point in my life when I thrived off this type of attention. I needed to feel seen. I needed to be noticed. I needed these things because I was lonely and insecure.

I do not think I am the only one with this desire. It often starts when we are young; little girls will often say, "Watch me daddy!" I remember when my brother learned how to jump in the pool during summer when he was little, he would run to the edge and always yell, "Watch this mom!"

Our thirst to be seen explains the popularity of social networking. We want others to know us. So we take multiple selfies, and see how many likes we can collect. But do we really genuinely like to be seen? Do you think everybody's profiles on social media are real? Do you think anybody ever poses a false self? Many of us, in the end, are a paradox: we want to be seen, but not that well. Don't get too close...Keep your distance please.

If you're anything like I used to be, I wanted you to know who I was but I did not want you to get too close.

I tried that before.

It was just too risky.

If you did not like me, then what?

With this mindset, I often entered into relationships by tiptoeing through many "get to know you" stages and never actually got to know anyone fully. But I learned that Jesus doesn't let us do that…Jesus does not allow us to build walls up around ourselves.

My life was changed when I was introduced to two women at a well who revealed this truth. We find the first woman in John 4, I encourage you to stop and take time to read about her. Before we discuss her, let's take a quick look at another woman at the well.

Abraham is the main character of this Bible story in early Genesis. He is a nomad from the east. God promised Abraham that He would make a great nation if he left his homeland and wandered to the land that God selected. This promise is found in Genesis 12:1-3. The Old Testament takes us through this promise. Abraham leaves home and wanders through a strange land with his clan, waiting on the promise. We see that Abraham accepted the promise of a son, but like many of us, he didn't wait for God to fulfill His word in His own time and in His own way. So we watch as his faith in God is tested. God's promise depends upon Abraham having a son, if Abraham never has a son, then how is God going to keep the promise? Ten years have passed since the original promise. Ten years of waiting, roaming, and wandering. We watch as Sarah, who is faithfully following Abraham becomes impatient. She comes up with a great idea (or so she thinks) and rushes God's plan.

Sarah has a servant girl named Hagar and suggests to Abraham, *"Go into my servant. It may be that I shall obtain children by her." I* remember reading this and thinking, "what in the world was going on in her mind? This is going to go well...NOT... This situation has disaster all over it." Just like we can't turn away from a train wreck, we keep reading and in Genesis 16:3, Abraham agrees to go into Hagar and she becomes pregnant. When that happened, Sarah became dishonored in Hagar's eyes. Sarah notices and becomes angry and confronts Abraham.

Abraham tells her, *"Do as you please,"* so Sarah did, whatever she wanted, and Hagar ran away. If we turn to Genesis 16:7-13 we see that she made her way to the desert, and the Angel of the Lord found her by a well

"Hagar, Sarai's maid, where have you come from, and where are you going?" The Angel asked. She said "I am fleeing from the presence of my mistress Sarai." The Angel told Hagar to go back to Sarai's tent. He told Hagar to submit to Sarah. He gave her a promise attached to the son in her womb, a promise that had a whiff of Abraham's promise in it.

One of my mom's favorite thing to do was watch my brother play sports. I remember once, sitting in the hospital bed with mom and she was so mad that she was going to miss my brothers basketball game. My dad came up with the idea to Facetime my mother during the game. The entire time my dad kept the viewfinder on my brother, so my mom was able to watch.

I think we can learn a lot about God by paying attention to who He keeps in the center of the view-finder in the text of scripture—In this moment, look how God tracks the movement of a pregnant slave girl in His viewfinder (Poe, 2013).

Did you catch what Hagar called the Angel of the Lord? *"The God who sees."*

The well, Beer-lahai-roi: means the well of the living one who sees. Can I suggest that, until that moment, nobody had seen Hagar? She is sitting there by the spring of water in the wilderness scared and homeless. An Egyptian girl caught or bought by a Mesopotamian family doing whatever she had to do to get by. She was just obeying orders to stay alive and then... when she did exactly as she was told, her master hates her for it. She was alone. She had no family. She could not make a call. She was completely by herself. She was pretty much disposable. They handled her like an appliance. Once she was used up, she became useless, just in the way trash is discarded. She was invisible. Nobody asked what she wanted, nobody cared how she felt, nobody knows who she really is.

Have you ever felt like this? Have you ever wondered if there is there anybody who sees? Anybody who knows your worth?

I know I have.

However, after reading about these two women, I have come to realize that: Yes, there is One who notices us. When the Angel talked to Hagar, He began like this: *"Hagar, Sarai's maid...."* The Angel knew her name. He knew *exactly* who she was! Are you surprised? That the One who scooped out the seas, heaped up the mountains, flung out the stars, painted the deserts, and colored the forest would notice Hagar? That the One who created a plot to save humanity, would help save a single girl caught in a domestic mess? That the One bothered by all our prayers would bother with a pregnant runaway? Are you really surprised? I was.

We are told in Matthew 10:30: *"Even the very hairs on your head are numbered."*

And that he *"counts our tears,"* In Psalms 56:8

He counts our steps *"For His eyes are upon the ways of a man, and He sees all his steps"* (Job 34:21).

Psalm 139-7-13 says

Where can I go from Your Spirit?
Or where can I flee from Your presence?
If I ascend into heaven, You are there;
If I make my bed in hell, behold, You are there.

If I take the wings of the morning,
And dwell in the uttermost parts of the sea,
Even there Your hand shall lead me,
And Your right hand shall hold me.
If I say, "Surely the darkness shall cover me, and the light about me be night, even the darkness is not dark to you; the night is bright as the day, for darkness is as light with you. For you formed my inward parts; you knitted me together in my mother's womb."

We cannot hide from God, so *why* do we hide from each other? Let's look at another woman at a well.

In traveling from Judea to Galilee, many of the Jews went completely around Samaria, for the Jews had nothing to do with the Samaritans; But, in John 4, we learn that Jesus went through Samaria and stopped at Jacob's well to refresh himself.

As Jesus sat down by a well, a Samaritan woman came to draw water and he began a conversation with her. It resulted not only in her following Jesus, but if you read vs 41 we see that it resulted in many others also becoming His disciples. Before we get to vs 41, let's look at verse, 16:

Jesus says, *"Go, call your husband."*

Why do you think he said this?

"Go, call your husband and come here," Jesus said.

"I have no husband," the woman said.

"You're right. You've had five. The man you're living with now is not your husband."

Jesus already knew that she had 5 husbands, that she currently "has a man," that is not her husband. A man that may not love her enough to marry her, and may be using her. We are ignorant of the details, their living arrangements, his intentions, and any circumstances. Jesus already knows, but He asks her anyway. Jesus picks out this woman's flaw, her biggest hurt, and pokes it. He didn't say, *"Oh, I am so sorry, you probably don't want to talk about that do you?"*

And when she answered, *"I have no husband,"* which was correct, did Jesus leave it?

For some reason, I imagine my grandmother as Jesus' wife... He would have heard it from her all the way back home from church...

"Why...did...you...ask...that?" (Swatting him on the shoulder between each word). Don't you have any sense at all? That was so embarrassing."

But Jesus doesn't care.. Jesus spelled it out in specific language, in case there was any doubt.

Why do you think he did this?

Why hurt her where she hurts?

Why poke her wound?

Why does Jesus find the one thing she doesn't want to talk about and demand to talk about it?

I think He would do the same thing with you and I..

Where is *your* wound? No, I don't mean the scar on your elbow from your bike wreck at age 11.

I mean your wound, you know, the one that is still open, the one that still hurts, the old one, the one that won't heal.

Where is it? Where is your hurt?

What is the one thing you would never want to talk about because I think that is the one thing that Jesus would demand to talk to you about.

Whatever Jesus did worked, if we look at the outcome of the encounter between Him and the woman at the well. We see in John 4:28

"So the woman left her water jar and went away into town and said to the people, "Come see a man who told me all that I ever did. Can this be the Christ?"

She said that as if it was a good thing. *"Come and see!"*

I would have probably said, uhhh "Run and hide!" "He is coming, and he knows *everything*!" Instead of running and hiding, my desire throughout this book is to say, "come see the man who saw me, and quenched my life thirst!"

This knowledge of being seen by God has quenched my thirst for attention and has helped me more effectively evangelize. This topic of being seen affects us in many ways, especially as women. I am going to ask a question that many reading this will probably not approve of, but why do we have such a hard time talking about our past struggles with one another? It is like we wear nice clothes on Sunday morning and pretend like we have it all together.

It seems as though we pretend that we are not all broken or thirsty inside. It is as if we build walls around ourselves and put on fake smiles.

I once told someone that I will always be open about my struggles, so I can show the way Christ has pulled me through those tough times. That individual replied: "Megan the less people know about you, the better." But, Paul did not have this mindset at all, he said *"The saying is trustworthy and deserving of full acceptance, that Christ Jesus came into the world to save sinners, of whom I am the foremost"* in 1 Timothy 1:15. He did not hide his struggles.

I do not agree with "the less people know the better." I do not agree with wearing our Sunday's best and pretending to have it all together. I think that is a trick of Satan to keep our relationships superficial because he knows the church is dangerous when the members become too unified.

We are told to *"bear one another's burdens"* (Galatians 6:2). How can we do this if we do not know one another's burdens? I'll admit, writing this book feels a lot like standing in the middle of a public place in my underwear. Perhaps someone will hold certain parts of these written words against me one day, but I am revealing myself anyways. I am doing this because I think Satan's biggest tactic is to convince us that no one needs to know

our problems. He convinces us that there are too many "gossips" in the church or people that just want to see us fail. But I do not think this is the truth. Yes, there are gossips in the church, but did this stop Jesus from bringing to light people's problems in front of others? Did that stop God from detailing every inch of David's thirsty life? What if God would have only included David's superficial parts and left out the details of him sinning and needing a solution? Would we have anyone in the Bible to relate to? I think this writer put it well when he states
"Confessing one's sins to someone – even someone we trust – is never easy because it means becoming vulnerable; it means admitting we need help. In a world that exalts individual achievement and despises weakness, revealing one's sins to another feels extremely uncomfortable. Then there is the fear of gossip which can so quickly circulate, especially in tight-knit Christian groups. But all this can be an excuse; a cop-out for not really turning away from sin. Hiding behind our Christianity, we keep our sin secret, not because we feel forgiven but because we fear wounded pride. Self-righteousness and the desire to look good have become so entrenched in us that instead of being the sinners we are, we lock ourselves behind a spiritual facade of our own making – a prison that keeps us isolated from each other and from God," (Fransham, 2018).

I am not implying that we need to stand in front of the congregation and air out our dirty laundry. What I am suggesting is that you never know who you can help by revealing your sin or past struggle. I cannot tell you how many times I have been encouraged by older women in the congregation who were not afraid to talk about their struggles with one another. It helped me understand that you do not have to be perfect to be a Christian.

I hope this week helps you realize that the only valuable attention we get comes from Jesus. He knows you and He knows everything you have done and everything you will do, yet He died for you regardless! This knowledge helped me to quench my thirst for attention and I hope it lessens your thirst as well.

Thirst Quenching Questions

When it comes to wanting attention, whose attention are you currently seeking?

Read Psalm 34:18; do you truly believe this?

yes

Is there a wound in your life you are trying to hide? Write it here and reflect on it.

How can understanding that God see's and knows us, help you overcome this wound?

Dig into the Bible for ways to overcome this wound. Write what you have found here.

Proverbs 28:13; whoever conceals his transgressions will not prosper, but he who confesses and forsakes them will obtain mercy." Are you concealing any sins? not from God

Read James 5:16; "Therefore, confess your sins to one another and pray for one another, that you may be healed. The prayer of a righteous person has great power as it is working." From this verse, what is the result of confessing your sins?

What holds you back from discussing your struggles with other sisters in Christ? pride, embarrassment

Read Ephesians 4:29; how can we use this to avoid being like those mentioned in 2 Corinthians 12:20? get rid of sins don't carry sinful burdens, be an example of a Child of God.

Week Six : Thirsty for Acceptance

My little children, I am writing these things to you so that you may not sin. But if anyone does sin, we have an advocate with the Father, Jesus Christ the righteous. 1 John 2:1

No one wakes up one day and says to themselves, "I think I will overdose on drugs and go to the hospital today." It is the result of a seed that was once planted and watered over time.

I once took an advanced pathophysiology class and realized that the more I learn about the human body, the more spiritual application I see. Take allergies for example. Did you know that clinical desensitization to allergens can be achieved in some people? Small quantities of the allergen are injected in increasing doses over a prolonged period of time. This procedure may reduce the severity of the allergic reaction in the treated individual (McCance and Huether, 2014).

I cannot help but wonder if this is what Satan did to me and still attempts to do today. Growing up, he slowly injected views of the world by one relationship at a time, one song at a time, one TV show at a time, one discouragement at a time, and slowly caused me to become desensitized towards the view of world.

Growing up, my parents spent time planting a seed in me. They watered that seed by making sure I was at Bible class on Sunday's and Wednesday's and church camp during the summer. For that I am thankful, because I think that is part of the reason I eventually came to Christ.

Throughout high-school and up until I was 23 and watched my mother die, the faith my parents had tried so hard to build in me was slowly being uprooted and replaced with the thirst to be accepted by my peers.

In this chapter I need to explain the harm that can occur from the company you keep and the desire to be accepted by the wrong people. I will warn you that this chapter goes a bit in detail. My goal is to paint a picture for you of the life I was living and take you through a walk in my shoes. Young or old, I hope you can relate to the negative impact that poor choices and bad influences can have on your life.

When I started growing into my Christianity, I fully believed that my life would be transformed through Christ Jesus and His word and I was on fire. I came up with a plan. The first step? Staying away from bad people, alcohol, and other temptation. Once I started reflecting on the importance of the company I kept, I started thinking back to my history and choice of friends.

It was clear that throughout my life, the company I kept and the thirst for attention and acceptance impacted my actions, my choices, and my purity.

Lets go back to Summer of 2006, when it all started for me.

On a rainy day, I texted Jacob to see what he was up to. I was restless as always and wanted to hang out because Jacob always found something fun to do. He showed up to my house and the raindrops sprinkled on my shoulder as I walked towards his car. I heard the sound of the windshield wipers going back and forth as I opened the car door and climbed in the front seat. While getting ready that day, I left my hair wet and tried a new eyeshadow on for blue eyes. Of course, as soon as I got in the car he said "Look at you and your big beautiful doe eyes."

Jacob always had a way of making me feel good, even though I wasn't attracted to him.

When we arrived to Jacob's barn, Jacob's friend Jessie was smoking something wrapped in paper and snorted some type of white powder. Jacob's barn had become our hang out place that year.

"What is that?" I asked.

"It's weed and coke, you've never tried it? You're missing out." Jessie responded

"No thanks, I'm not into that." I replied

"I thought you said you would try anything once?" Jacob chimed in. "Maybe later," I replied.

And so grew the seed of temptation. The devil is tricky, he

does not come at you red faced and horns, he comes disguised as pleasure.

That seed continued to grow and flourish throughout high school. While it grew, other temptations were planted.

You know those sweet words a young girl tells herself:

"I will save it."

I had every intention of saving my virginity for marriage, but Satan knows what he is doing through high school peers. I remember the day it happened while we were waiting for class to start, the boys in class were cracking jokes about the party that weekend, and how many girls they would get with that night at the Halloween party.

"I'm saving myself for marriage," I replied.

"Yea, right you'll lose it in college, there's no way," Ross said sarcastically.

Later that day at my locker, my friend Gretchen came up to me and said, "Girl, you have to come to the party tonight. Just tell your mom to call and talk to my mom, but we will have my sister pretend like she is my mom and she will lie for us."

My mom was one of the strict ones. She had this rule that wherever I went, she had to speak to the parents of whoever I was hanging out with. I loathed this rule and I was sure to find ways around it.

Mom called, and Gretchen's sister pretended; mom bought the lie and I arrived at the party. But, I felt out of place. This was a popular kid party, and even though I was friends with the popular kids, I never quite related to them. Something always made me feel out of place, I could never put my finger on it.

I bumped into my friend Dana, who also felt out of place. She yelled over the music, "Hey, Jacob is having people over, do you want to go?" I nodded, "Yes, please! I've gotta get out of here."

And so I found myself in the car with Dana on the way to

Jacob's.

My boyfriend and I got in a fight that night. He had been ignoring me and hanging out with another girl. I knew he cheated on me all the time, but I didn't care. He was popular, a wrestler, had anger problems, and I felt like I needed to be there for him. Previously mentioned, my choice in guys never the best; I always chose the bad boys.

Jacob had become my best friend. As soon as we had arrived to Jacob's I could tell he had been drinking.

Fed up with being uncomfortable, I broke and said:
"Okay, Jac, I want to drink!"
Surprised, because I was a "good girl," Jacob led me to the refrigerator and pulled out a bottle of Bacardi 151.

"Ever had this?" He smiled, with a mischievous smile.

"No, but I'll try anything once," I replied with a curious smile. For some reason, I hated being known as a "good girl," so I started to rebel against that reputation. Jacob had also started developing feelings for me, but I always pretended not to notice.

I found myself thinking back to earlier that day when Mom was washing the dishes, looking out the window as Jacob pulled up to the driveway in his red truck and said,
"That boy has it bad for you."
I rolled my eyes and said, "No he doesn't, we are just friends Mom."
I just liked to kill time with him and enjoyed his company.

After one too many shots of Bacardi 151, I found myself laying in the grass with the whole world spinning. I kept calling my boyfriend, but he didn't answer. So, I threw my flip phone across the yard.

Jacob came out angrily and said "You're calling him again? Just come inside!"

I giggled and told him I felt like I couldn't move. So he scooped me up and carried me inside and laid me on the floor in the small house by the barn. I found myself slowly drifting off to sleep, but was woken by the sensation of Jacob's hand unbuttoning the top button of my jeans. "He will stop, I told myself." I felt my pants keep coming undone, and felt a pain I had never felt before, but I couldn't move. The rest is a blur.

Early the next morning, Dana dropped me off at my parents and before I got out of the car asked if everything was okay. "I just feel weird," I said. "And it hurts down there." I felt a discomfort I had never felt before.

I slowly started realizing my innocence was gone. That thing I was going to save until marriage... Gone.

Every day I came home from school, I would drop my backpack off and go to my room to be alone.

I didn't know what to think, or how to feel.

I worked at Texas Roadhouse that summer as a hostess. A few days after this at work, I found myself in the bathroom talking to Sally. "Well, it could have been my fault, I mean, I did drink and I sort of remember, I didn't stop him. I couldn't move."

Sally said, "Girl this is not your fault." Her words were comforting, but I still felt guilty.

At school that week, I was eaten up with guilt. I stood in the hallway of high school and told my boyfriend what happened. He slammed his fist against the locker and started walking fast and angrily. He was headed to confront Jacob in the cafeteria.

"Is it true?"

He pushed Jacob on the chest, Jacob backed up a few feet and the whole cafeteria looked at them.

"No, that's not how it happened bro."

Totally embarrassed, I ran into the bathroom, sitting on top of the toilet, I pulled my legs to my chest. I overheard two girls talking, one girl to the other: " I can't believe someone would lie about being raped, what a horrible person."

Crushed, I waited until they left and walked out of the bathroom and walked fast down the hall. I survived that day of school and went home to find my parents sitting at the kitchen table. I always knew something serious was going on when they sat at the kitchen table. I received a ton of lectures in the confines of those chairs.

"Your principal called today and told us what happened. Honey, why didn't you tell us?" Dad sad.

I just sat there in silence with my arms crossed.

"We want you to go to counseling," Mom said.

"What? No way. Why? It was just a mistake, I'm not even sure it was his fault. I put myself in that situation. I am not even sure what really happened!"

Sadly, this happens often in high school. Boys and girls are enticed towards alcohol and lose their innocence. Not realizing the power of the company they keep. Not realizing the impact of alcohol and peer pressure. Not realizing that yes, "bad" girls seem like they are having fun, but there is always consequences to poor choices. The need to be accepted rules over all these other things.

There are multiple things that may happen when a girl is taken advantage of.

1. She completely shuts down and pushes away every boy she meets, building walls around herself in fear that someone will hurt her.

2. She settles in a toxic relationship, becoming overly sexual and too insecure to believe she deserves better.

I became a mix of both.

In addition, after I had lost my innocence, I no longer cared about keeping it. Sadly, this is a common occurrence in high school. No matter what age we are, it is extremely hard for girls, and women to stay sexually pure, especially after something tragic happens. Why? These were my reasons, maybe they are yours too:

1. Peer pressure
2. Hating the reputation of being "the good girl," because bad girls seemed to have more fun and get more boys.
3. Loving my boyfriend.
4. Not understanding why I need to wait?
5. Not being in love with God and totally devoted to staying pure and committed to him
6. Rushing God's timing.
7. Not believing I was worth the wait, or that any guy would wait for me.

Peer pressure is such a tough subject to conquer. The Bible is amazing because it is filled with knowledge we need. In attempt to conquer peer pressure, lets take a moment to study a few verse in Psalm 1:

"Blessed is the man
who walks not in the counsel of the wicked,
nor stands in the way of sinners,
nor sits in the seat of scoffers;
but his delight is in the law of the Lord,
*and on his law he meditates day and night."*Psalm 1:1-2

In this verse it says *"Blessed is the man who walks not in the counsel of the wicked."* As young women, we want to be accepted, we want to relate to others, and we want to have a connection. This causes us to often take advice from our worldly friends, magazine articles, or famous people that seem like they have their life together even if they are not living for God. But in this verse, God is telling us to do the opposite. In the Bible the word "walk" is a description of lifestyle (WVBS, 2014). Counsel is a word that means "advice." So in this text it is saying we are blessed if we do not take the advice from the ungodly. This is hard to do when our friends seem to be succeeding by following their own worldly advice. But as Jesus says, this is the *"blind leading the blind"* (Matthew 15:14). This doesn't change as we get older. It is so important to surround ourselves with Godly friends.

In the second verse of this Psalm it reads *"who walks not in the counsel of the wicked."* This reminds me of the verse in 1 Thessalonians 5:22 that reads *"flee every appearance of evil."* This is very difficult, but we are promised that we will be blessed if we succeed.

I often try and pay close attention to the company I keep because of my history of choosing poorly. Helpful questions I ask myself are:

1. What type advice are they offering me? If it is Godly advice, am I taking it, or becoming defensive? Typically when I respond defensively to advice or suggestions instead of humbly, it is because I know it is something I struggle with. If it is not Godly advice, should I listen?

2. What can I learn from them? It could be a lesson or a blessing. I used to have this mentality where I wanted to learn from my own mistakes. But please listen when I tell you, there is so much relief in learning from the mistakes of others! It is so much less painful. Listening to advice older women in the church have to offer can be so beneficial because chances are, they have experienced something that taught them that lesson.

3. What type of fruit is in their life? Some people are very good with words, but when it comes to results, they have nothing to show. People with good habits will produce good fruit in their

lives.

The influence of the company we keep can often make or break us (1 Corinthians 15:33).

My thirst for acceptance once negatively impacted my life. It impacted the type of attention I wanted, the type of person I dated, the way I acted, the friends I chose, and the decisions I made. After reflecting on my history of poor choices and reliving the heartache that seeking the wrong type of acceptance had on my life, I was able to grow and learn from it. Now the acceptance I want is that of God and godly influences. It has made a complete difference in my life and behavior. I am confident it will do the same for you.

Thirst Quenching Questions

Reflect on your life, have you been thirsty for bad boys, attention, or acceptance? Write about it here.

Read Exodus 32; what was the result of the people peer pressuring Aaron?

Have you ever been impacted by peer pressure? Using Scripture, what measures can you take to overcome this?

Who are the five most important people in your life? Do you find qualities of those people in yourself?

Do you need to prune any of those people out of your life? List those people here, pray for them, and then work to distance yourself. This will not be easy, but when you rid every bad influence you release from your life, God will bless you with new friends.

Read 1 John 2:16; what are the three pleasures listed? Who do these pleasures come from?

Have any of the pleasures caused a negative impact in your life?

In Matthew 4:10, how did Jesus combat the prince of this world?

Read James 4:7; how can we resist the devil?

In Psalm 119:11; what did the psalmist store/hide in his heart so he would not sin?

According to this verse what can we store in our hearts to combat peer pressure and pleasures of the world?

What type of acceptance are you seeking?

"Wherefore the rather, brethren, give diligence to make your calling and election sure: for if ye do these things, ye shall never fall: For so an entrance shall be ministered unto you abundantly into the everlasting kingdom of our Lord and Savior Jesus Christ." 2 Peter 1:10-11

After I conquered my thirst for an identity, bad boys, attention, and acceptance, I began to be thirsty for a purpose. I understood that God knew me, and made me, but I had a burning passion to know why. But, there was something in the way of discovering my true purpose as a Christian: I was struggling to believe that I was good enough for the gospel. Throughout this chapter we will be exploring discouragement and how it can impact our purposes as Christians.

The beach is the place where I feel closest to God. The ocean is so big and it reminds me of how small I am and how large God is. Once on a vacation, I was walking along the beach, while my aunt was searching through seashells, I noticed that she and the people around, and even me, were quick to throw the broken or chipped seashells away. You see, everyone wants the bright and beautiful, non-chipped or broken seashells. So the ones that don't make the cut, the cracked, chipped, or mediocre ones, are thrown back with the others. I thought to myself, "I am a lot like those cracked sea shells; nothing is different about me. Maybe I haven't been tossed and turned in the sea, but I have definitely been broken, bruised and chipped, from this storm we call life."

Like those thrown away seashells, I often feel broken. There was a time in my life when the feeling of brokenness stood in the way of Christianity. I looked strong on the outside, but felt tired, numb and apathetic on the inside. In scripture, Satan is referred to as "the father of lies." Satan once slithered into mind and said, *"You're nothing but a broken shell Megan; boring, insignificant... You're not good enough to live the Christian life."* "Plus, you're missing out on all the fun, look at your old friends, just look how much fun they are having. You can't do this, who are you trying to fool?" For awhile, I believed this and became discouraged. This mindset caused me to keep members of the church at arm's length. I found that I related more to my worldly friends because I knew more about their lives and they seemed just as broken as I was. I began to crave hanging out with them and living my old life style. So I started to question why I became a Christian.

In the words of Michael Shank (2014), "No one decides to leave the Lord overnight. Leaving the Lord usually happens in small, incremental steps."

When we decide to obey the gospel, we are initially excited, zealous, and eager to make the commitment to surrender our lives to Jesus Christ. But some days we may feel far away from Him. Maybe this is why you picked up this book. What causes this? I think the answer is that we spiritually dehydrate ourselves. We learn from scripture that the Word of God is the essential food for the life of one's soul. *It is living water* (John 4:10, 14), *milk* (1 Peter 2:2), *bread* (John 6:33) *strong meat* (Hebrews 5:12) and sweeter than *honey* (Psalms 119:103). The soul becomes dehydrated without it, and when something is dehydrated long enough, it dies. When our faith dies, reverting to our old selves and our old ways is an easy transition, it is the default mode (Shank, 2014).

I always love attending church camp because you get to see a fire re-lit in young and old Christian lives. Everyone leaves feeling uplifted. It is easy to put on Christ there because everyone around you is doing the same. I have witnessed many young girls repent from their previous behavior during camp. They become more involved in the youth group when they return to their home congregations. But when summer ends and school begins, these same young people who were so on fire for Christ, start to lose their heat. They become entrenched with the influence of their non-Christian peers and their faith becomes diluted. Eventually, they lose their purpose as a Christian because life outside of Christ begins to feel like the norm. They neglect to feed their souls with the Word of God because they are overwhelmed with homework and pursuing a career in this world. I know this, because I was once one of those young people. Now, as a volunteer nurse at camp the past three years, I have witnessed this process happen over and over. So what happens to cause us to lose our fire for Christ and a desire for a purpose as a Christian?

During my trip to the beach I mentioned before, I discovered the answer to stopping this process: focus less on ourselves and more on God. When we focus on ourselves and defining our own purpose in life, discouragement sets in because we forget why we were created. At church camp, the primary purpose is to grow as a Christian and learn how to spread the gospel. The campers spend time memorizing Bible verses and there is a devotion each evening and one in each cabin at night. We are immersed in God's word and it changes our hearts and passions. It is when we neglect this process, that spiritual dehydration occurs.

In a previous chapter, I asked you about 2 Timothy 3:16. In this verse, we learn that God chose to communicate with us through words. It says:

"All Scripture is breathed out by God and profitable for teaching, for reproof, for correction, and for training in righteousness." This is a verse I recommend committing to memory because it is so important. Another verse that I recommend committing to memory is Hebrews 4:12. It reads: *"For the word of God is living and active, sharper than any two-edged sword, piercing to the division of soul and of spirit, of joints and of marrow, and discerning the thoughts and intentions of the heart."* It is so easy to forget that God's word is living and active and meant for teaching, reproof, correction, and training in every day life. For me, this happens when I am not studying His word and not involved in His church. I begin to doubt myself as a Christian and lose the desire to spread the gospel because I forget my purpose on earth. This world starts to feel like my home, and the thought of heaven seems distant. I get caught up in the moment.

I believe I have found the answer to breaking this cycle of thinking and it begins with returning to our Bibles. Returning to our Bible's show us that this life is not about finding our own purpose, it is about pursuing God's purpose. We were made for His glory (Isaiah 43:6-7).When our purpose becomes to give God the glory and seek and save the lost, there is no time to keep focusing on ourselves.

There is a real battle going on right now. Satan is out to steal, kill, and destroy as many souls as possible. God's purpose is to save as many souls as possible. In 2 Corinthians 4:4-6 we read: "*the god of this world has blinded the minds of the unbelievers, to keep them from seeing the light of the gospel of the glory of Christ, who is the image of God. For what we proclaim is not ourselves, but Jesus Christ as Lord, with ourselves as your servants for Jesus' sake. For God, who said, "Let light shine out of darkness," has shone in our hearts to give the light of the knowledge of the glory of God in the face of Jesus Christ."*
Satan is blinding the mind of unbelievers by keeping them ignorant of God's word and of the gospel. Our purpose is to be the lights that draw people closer to God and help them to see that He does not want anyone to perish, but all to reach repentance (2 Peter 3:9).

Many of us get so caught up in pursuing our own purpose in life that we forget who we are really here for. Or we become so paralyzed by the pain and suffering or mistakes we have made that it makes us feel unfit for the task. In my eighth-grade art class, I had this art teacher who made us do a project in permanent marker. We were not aloud to erase our mistakes, instead we had to incorporate our mistakes into our piece of art. I think that's what God does. He doesn't completely take away the pain or mess of our mistakes, one of his laws is that we reap what we sow (Galatians 6) but he does have a way of taking our mistakes and turning them out to be something that can be used to glorify Himself.

Maybe like me, you feel like you are full of mistakes, incapable of reaching your potential, or wondering if you even have a purpose. Perhaps, you feel as if you have nothing to offer. Feeling thirsty for purpose has caused me to discover that the beautiful thing about being in a relationship with God, is that he gives us a plan for not quitting this Christian journey:

2 Peter 1:10-11

"Wherefore the rather, brethren, give diligence to make your calling and election sure: for if ye do these things, ye shall never fall: For so an entrance shall be ministered unto you abundantly into the everlasting kingdom of our Lord and Savior Jesus Christ.

This plan works because giving diligence to our calling prevents apathy. When we invest our time and energy into doing something for the Lord, our apathy evaporates. What are we giving diligence to? Making our calling and election sure (Shank, 2014). Developing Christ like qualities. In this way, God gives us direction and purpose. When we have direction and purpose, we become excited. So what are these things Peter mentions we should give diligence to? "*And beside this, giving all diligence, add to your faith virtue, and to virtue knowledge; and to knowledge temperance; and to temperance patience, and to patience godliness; and to godliness brotherly kindness; and to brotherly kindness charity.* (1 Peter 1:5-7).

Our purpose as Christians is pursuing, developing and mastering Christ's virtues and spreading His gospel. This is a long lifetime pursuit... But, guess what? Life is short...

James 4:14 "*What is your life? For you are a mist that appears for a little time and then vanishes.*" As long as we are trying, repenting when we mess up, turning away from our mistakes, and trying again, the blood of Christ cleanses us continually.. Remember, it says so in 1 John 1:9 *"If we confess our sins to him, he is faithful and just to forgive us our sins and to cleanse us from all wickedness."*

Thirst Quenching Questions

What does a thirst for purpose look like in your life?

Read Proverbs 19:21; who's purpose should we be focused on?

Are you pursuing a purpose in the world or a purpose in the kingdom of God?

Read 2 Timothy 1:8-9; what are we to share in? What are we to share in it for?

Read Psalm 119:1-11 and reflect.

How can applying these verses provide us with purpose or change our purpose?

Read Philippians 2:12-13; what does it mean to work out your salvation with fear and trembling?

What are some ways to accomplish this?

Read Job 1 and 2; in what ways did Satan tempt Job?

In Job 2:3;what qualities did the Lord say Job possessed?

How can we obtain these same qualities as Christians?

What is your current method of memorizing the scriptures?

Check out scripturetyper.com for some helpful ways!

Read Mark 16:15; what should we be doing with gospel?

What does spreading the gospel currently look like in your life?

Week Eight: Thirsty for an Adventure

"And he said to them, "Go into all the world and proclaim the gospel to the whole creation." Mark 16:15

I have always had a taste for adventure. In fact, I joined the military right after high school because I wanted to travel and explore. But once I started living for Jesus and my thirst for purpose was quenched, my eyes were opened to a new adventure. A satisfying adventure. A year or so after I was fully dedicated to my Christian walk, I found myself really thinking about the words: *"And he said to them, "Go into all the world and proclaim the gospel to the whole creation,"* Mark 16:15 and felt a thirst to accomplish this. So I decided to make plans to go on a mission trip. After my first mission trip, I fell completely in love with the idea of becoming a missionary and spreading the gospel. I was still in the Air National Guard at the time and I was forced to make a decision, stay in and retire, accepting a new position with higher pay and a higher title, or end my enlistment.

I decided to finish my last year in the military and resign my position. I was so conflicted because when I asked advice from my family, they told me to pursue my career. It took me a while to decide, but after a lot of prayer and patience, I ended my enlistment. My family was not happy but they supported my decision. I decided to be an officer in the Lord's army. As with military missions, each mission trip involved lots of planning I acquired information, established relationships, discussed options and dates and then raised funds to set out on my first mission trip to India. I was asked to teach first aid and emergency childbirth to a group of women at a Bible school in Assam, India.

After this trip, I was drawn to traveling and seeing God's church around the world, so in 2016, I joined a medical mission trip serving in the Philippines. I was again expecting to use my nursing skills as I had done in India. On this trip, we were there to work with the new congregation that had been planted, Reina Mercedes church of Christ. The local preacher and his wife, Edmar and Airlyn, were awaiting our arrival. They are a young zealous couple in their twenties, on fire for the Lord. Dale Byrum and his wife, Karen, were the missionary couple who had organized this mission trip. I met Dale at our home congregation when he did a report on his work in the Philippines. I was instantly drawn to the work he was doing and walked up to him, introduced myself and asked if I could join his trip. The rest is history.

When we arrived to the Philippines, I was ready to help with nursing, but to my surprise, Dale told me he had different plans for me. During this medical mission, he wanted me to teach the adult women the gospel. He explained that he believed there is power with women teaching other women the gospel. He believes that there is an emotional bond we are able to create with one another. I was terrified. I felt like Moses when God asked him to save His people. Like Moses, I felt completely unqualified to do the task being asked of me. I was comfortable helping others by using my nursing skills because I am trained in the medical profession. But teaching people the gospel? This was new for me. It made me feel vulnerable, and I did not like feeling this insecurity.

The first day of the mission, I was completely discouraged. I watched the Filipino nurses medically treat the other Filipinos, I was jealous of them and wanted so much to help people physically. I did not know where to begin when it came to one-on-one evangelism, especially with women I hardly knew. I wanted to go home. I did not know where I fit in on this mission, and I started to feel alone and out of place. No one seemed to be interested in studying with me. When I returned to my hotel room that night, I prayed to God and apologized to Him for wanting to do things my way, and asked Him to use me in whatever way He needed me. I went to dinner later that night with my friend Rachael. Rachael and I are members of the same congregation in Ohio, and we decided to go on this trip together. Rachael told me that she felt like she did not belong on this trip. I felt as if God knew we needed to have that conversation.

Due to Rachel's willingness to be open about her struggles, I was able to tell Rachael that I felt the same, and told her about the prayer I prayed to overcome that feeling. It was a blessing to know that I was not alone, and that I had someone to struggle with.

On the second day in the Philippines, I sat again, waiting to begin personal studies with the willing Filipino women. On this day, I was to sit in a corner of the building where we were hosting our medical mission and wait for any woman that wanted to have a study after they had gone through the line to see the nurses and doctors for care. So I sat, and waited, feeling well out of my element. As time crawled by, I figured it would be another day that I failed to do the Lord's work, but then I watched as a Filipino woman, started approaching me. My heart dropped with anxiety. She had a comforting smile and was clearly eager to talk to me. When she reached my area, she smiled and said "I want to have a Bible study." Airlyn, was my translator for the day, and with her assistance we were able to study the word together. I was so nervous that I was going to say the wrong thing.

Anna Liza was the name of this woman and she had a son named Jayden who was just a toddler. I had brought candy in my backpack that day, so I smiled and handed him a sucker, and he crawled into my lap during the study. He eventually fell asleep in my lap. Since her son was comfortable, Anna Liza became more secure in talking with me. We discussed her family, her struggles, and religion. It turned out that she had taught her self English by watching English television shows. She was shy with speaking English so for the most part, Airlyn translated for her. After building a relationship, we eventually started discussing the gospel, God's church, and how to become part of it.

I asked Anna Liza to read Mark 16:15, she read *"Go into*

all the world and proclaim the gospel to the whole creation. Whoever believes and is baptized will be saved, but whoever does not believe will be condemned." Whenever I study with someone, I always have them read the Bible for themselves. I do this because when I was studying, I wanted to see things for myself. After all, it is not me who is doing the converting, it is the word of God.

I asked Anna Liza if she knew what the gospel was. She said no, but that she was interested in learning more. She explained that she was Roman Catholic but did not know why she was Roman Catholic. As Airlyn translated, my mind wandered back to a time when my mother was Roman Catholic before she was baptized into the Lord's church. I remember the day she was baptized, I was curious about what it meant to be a Christian then. I wish I knew then, what I know now.

When Airlyn was finished translating, I touched Anna Liza's knee and I told her that I wanted her to know that I came to the Philippines because I loved her and that I was apart of the Lord's church and that I came all the way from America because I have a job to do and that job is to show the love of Christ, by telling people about His Gospel. In that moment, I told the truth. I did love Anna Liza, and my job as a Christian was to obey the verse we had just read, Mark 16:15. So on this day, with our Bibles opened, we reviewed from the beginning when Eve bit into the fruit, bringing death upon us all. We discussed sin, and how it separates us from God and God's remedy for us. We discussed the fact that scripture says *"The Lord is not slow to fulfill his promise as some count slowness, but is patient toward you, not wishing that any should perish, but that all should reach repentance"* 2 Peter 3:9 and that God desires all to come to repentance, not just some people. We then discussed the church and the importance of commitment.

The most important truth that someone has to understand

about becoming a Christian is that it is not just about being baptized. Sure, baptism is what puts us in the church and saves us from our sins. But many people fail to understand that it is a life long commitment. As Anna Liza and I continued our study, I had her read John 3:16-17 which says *"For God so loved the world, that he gave his only Son, that whoever believes in him should not perish but have eternal life. For God did not send his Son into the world to condemn the world, but in order that the world might be saved through him."*

"How does this scripture say we are saved Anna Liza?" I asked. She said she did not know. "It says we are saved through God's son! Jesus!" I said excited. We do not have to pay a bunch of money or stand on our head or have some special talent, we just have to choose to love Him back and obey Him. We discussed how to get into Christ. We looked at the plan laid out in the scriptures for becoming a Christian. As we continued our study, I asked Anna Liza how many churches there are. She explained that there are so many denominations and that is confusing. I asked her to read Matthew 16:18-19, which states *"And I also say to you that you are Peter and on this rock I will build My church and the gates of Hades shall not prevail against it. And I will give you the keys of the kingdom of Heaven and whatever you bind on earth will be bound in heaven and whatever you loose on earth will be loosed in Heaven."* "Anna Liza, whose church did Jesus say that He would build?" I asked. She smiled and said "His church." So I asked her if He said that He would build multiple churches, and she smiled and said no.

I asked Anna Liza how we become part of the church. She said she did not know. My favorite thing about Bible study is allowing someone to answer their own questions with scripture. Watching a light bulb unveil inside their head as they realize the truth of the gospel is so rewarding. It reminds me of the day the light bulb was switched on in my head when I realized the truth.

We continued our study and we turned to Acts chapter two. As we read through this chapter we discussed how on that day God was and is still today calling sinners to repent and be baptized. We discussed what it means to be baptized and Anna Liza read Romans 6:1-6 which reads: *"What shall we say then? Are we to continue in sin that grace may abound? By no means! How can we who died to sin still live in it? Do you not know that all of us who have been baptized into Christ Jesus were baptized into his death? We were buried therefore with him by baptism into death, in order that, just as Christ was raised from the dead by the glory of the Father, we too might walk in newness of life. For if we have been united with him in a death like his, we shall certainly be united with him in a resurrection like his. We know that our old self was crucified with him in order that the body of sin might be brought to nothing, so that we would no longer be enslaved to sin."* We uncovered the fact that in order to become part of the Lord's church, we have to be in Christ. We also discussed that when we are baptized, we are baptized into Jesus's death and when we come up out of the water we walk in the newness of life. Then, we discussed the word baptism. We discussed the fact that Roman Catholics often sprinkle to baptize, but we must stop and remember what original languages the Bible is written in and what exactly the word baptism means.

At the end of the study with Anna Liza, I said "I am no one special, but I do know that God loves you, and I love you. It is my job as a Christian to tell you about God's church and show you from scripture how to join it. So, you read for yourself how to join, are you ready to become part of it?" Just like that, Anna Liza, with a big smile said, "Yes, I want to be baptized into the Lord's church!" I was so shocked and so excited that I could have cried.

However, I made sure Anna Liza understood that being baptized is not the only requirement, a life long commitment is required.

We see this in Revelation 2:10 *"Do not fear what you are about to suffer. Behold, the devil is about to throw some of you into prison, that you may be tested, and for ten days you will have tribulation. Be faithful unto death, and I will give you the crown of life."* Anna Liza said she understood this and was excited and ready. She continued studying with Edmar for a few minutes to verify that she actually understood this commitment to Christianity. Together, we all piled into a van and drove to the water park to baptize her. All the while I was questioning: Could it have been this simple? Do you simply teach God's word? In my heart I already had my answer. It sure was! I thought about Paul's writing, *"I planted, Apollos watered, but God gave the growth,"* (1 Corinthians 3:6). I was thankful for God giving the increase, but wondered who planted Anna Liza's seed. This was a perfect example of Paul's writing. Someone had planted Anna Liza's see, we watered it, and God gave the increase. The fact is that Anna Liza was searching for the truth and willing to read it for herself. She was seeking God with her whole heart and found Him!

Anna Liza is still a faithful member of the church today! I am not telling you about my experience to brag or boast in the things I have done for the Lord. I just want you to know that I discovered a satisfying adventure: spreading the gospel and this is what it looks like in my life.

You can be part of that satisfying adventure as well. It does not require you to leave the country, it just requires you to have a willing heart to work for the Lord and to spread His gospel.

At the end of this chapter, I listed questions that can be used in a Bible study with someone. I challenge you to invite a friend to have a Bible study with you and work through the questions together.

Thirst Quenching Questions

Read 2 Peter 3:16-7; how can we avoid twisting the scriptures?

Read 1 Peter 3:15; According to this verse, we should be able to defend our beliefs, yet with ______ and _______.

Respectfully, take a look at your life and read the words spoken by Jesus in Matthew 16:24; what do you find hardest about this?

Read Mark 16:15; what is this gospel?

Many people know John 3:16, but read John 3:17, how does this tell us we are saved?

Read 1 Corinthians 15:3-4. Why did Christ die and what did He according to?

Find and make a list of prophecies of Christ's death in the Old Testament. An example is Isaiah 53:3-6

Read Galatians 3:27; how does this tell us we get into Christ?

Read Romans 6:3-10; what were be baptized into? What should we consider ourselves dead to? Alive to?

Read Acts chapter Two: Write what happened in this chapter in your own words:

When they were pricked to the heart and asked Peter, "What shall we do?" What was Peter's response?

How were you baptized? Were you sprinkled? Immersed?

Look up the Greek word for baptism; what does it mean?

Why were you baptized? Compare this to Acts
2:28

Read 1 Peter 3:21; what does this tell us about baptism?

Read Acts 8:35, what did Philip preach to the Eunuch?

Why did the Eunuch want Philip to stop the chariot?

Read Acts 16: 25-40. What does vs 33 say they did at
once?

Read Matthew 4:17, what does it mean to repent?

Read Acts 16:31, what is a vital step before being baptized?

Compare these events with your Christian life, are the consistent? Why or Why not?

Read Acts 20:28, what did He purchase the church with?

Read Ephesians 1:22-23; what does it say the church is?

Read Ephesians 4:4, from this verse, how many bodies
What do these verses tell us in regards to how many churches there are?

What church do you belong to?

Does your church resemble the church found in the new testament?

Wrestle with your salvation and write a conclusion of your findings, defending your faith and
salvation using scripture:

Week Nine: Thirsty for Love

"If you love me, you will keep my commandments."
John 14:15

Once my thirst for an identity, attention, acceptance, and adventure was quenched, I found myself satisfied being a single woman of God. I started becoming more involved in my congregation and getting to know the other members. I kept myself busy growing spiritually and living for Christ. I spent time digging deep into Gods word to discover what He wanted from me. I was truly happy and truly satisfied. Then something happened, Luke Taylor caught my eye.

Luke and I had grown up in the same congregation, but I was too busy chasing bad boy's to ever notice him. But that all changed when I started being mentally present at worship. One year, I volunteered at church camp as the nurse. As I said in the previous chapter, I was drawn to church camp because it is an amazing place to grow as a Christian. During worship one night at camp, it was Luke's turn to preach and I sat in my chair in awe. I had no idea he could preach so well, and no idea he would preach on my every desire.

I will never forget when I leaned into my Aunt Tami during that night at worship and said "Is it possible for me to be in love with someone's soul?" He preached with such passion. He preached things I was feeling. His preaching made me feel like I wasn't crazy. It was as if he was reading my mind. He realized how important and how real the gospel is and how much work we had to do. Could he be too good to be true?

That year at church camp, Luke donated his hair during an auction, and my grandpa nominated me to be the one to shave his head. He even looked good bald. I had it bad for him. After church camp, I would see Luke at church and always think to myself he was so cute. I went to good news for youth event once (this is an event for young people in the church) and Luke preached on Elijah. Every time we made eye contact, he got a huge smile on his face and I could not stop smiling.

Maybe he liked me too?

The next year at church camp, I was sitting on the porch of the nurses cabin reading Esther, thinking to myself, "I feel so alone." I walked into the nurses cabin and prayed for someone to comfort me. I prayed for a friend. Then, I walked back out and continued to try and read. As I sat there, I heard *"How's the nurse doing?"* It was Luke, walking by with that charming smile of his. He walked up the steps to where I was sitting and sat with me, and we read the book of Esther together.

The amazing thing about pursuing God, is that He blows you away when you least expect it. As much as I did not want to admit it, I was thirsty for a godly love. Luke and I have known each other since we were little, however, I never really noticed him until I stopped chasing bad boys and started chasing God. My thirst for love would have never been filled if I had stayed focused on bad boys.

Luke and I eventually decided to get married. Four days after we were married I learned of my new diagnosis of breast cancer. This has caused many of our plans to be put on hold and has been a very trying experience. Although we struggle, I feel as if Luke and I could conquer anything because we started on a firm foundation.

The foundation we started on involved both of us being totally satisfied in God. We made Him our main priority. When we were dating, we were able to save sex for marriage. We did this by setting physical boundaries and by *lots* of prayer. On days when we were really attracted to each other, Luke would stop and say we need to pray. One thing that also helped, was that I told Luke if we messed up and had sex before marriage, I could never marry him. I told him that I wanted to obey God, and if I was dating someone that could not help me obey God with something as important as saving sex for marriage, then God would probably never trust us with something bigger. I think the thought of losing one another and the thought of disobeying God is what helped us stay pure.

Believe me when I tell you, it is worth the wait. Overcoming that temptation made us feel as if we could conquer anything together. Having someone totally devote themselves in a marriage covenant with you before you give yourself physically to them, is the most satisfying feeling. We devoted ourselves to God before we devoted ourselves to each other. In turn, we feel incredibly secure in our marriage. I know that Luke loves God more than me, which means he loves me properly. Scripture says, *"Husbands, love your wives, just as Christ loved the church and gave Himself up for her"* (Ephesians 5:25). In turn, when it comes time to submit to him in certain situations, I can do it confidently; knowing that he has our best interests at heart.

Every day I am experiencing a love from Luke that makes scripture come alive to me. Christ sacrificed Himself for the church, He denied Himself for the church. Luke obeys this example and in turn, I am blessed. From rubbing my back because he knows it distracts me from pain, to playing with my hair while I still have it, to washing and brushing my hair when I was too sore to. He still brings home flowers to brighten up my day. When I am having a rough day he says "I'm sorry you're going through this," instead of minimizing it by saying "at least you don't have this..." He is patient when I'm grumpy and still kisses me at every red light even though we made that tradition two years ago. He drains my two drains from the mastectomy and helps me track my medications. He even sacrifices a restful night sleep on the couch next to me because I currently have to sleep in a recliner. He shows me Christ daily and inspires and challenges me to be a better Christian. I am so thankful God placed him in my life.

I often pray for my bad qualities to be revealed in my life. Even though this is just the beginning of our journey with cancer, as well as the beginning of our marriage, I think I have been blessed with realizing some things about myself. As I sit and write this book, new struggles have been revealed in my mind. I have been struggling with vanity. Yes, I know everyone does, and that I am allowed to. But I'm writing this to young girls and women about the importance of knowing your beauty is not based on your outward appearance.

If you have instagram or Facebook, it is easy to get caught up in comparing yourself to other women. Many of these women appear to have perfect figures, perfect faces, and perfect hair. The other day I found myself envying another woman and thirsting after her beauty.

The thought of pieces of my body being removed and then having to have drains on my sides for two weeks and eventually lose my hair as a new wife, scared me. I was afraid that Luke wouldn't find me attractive, or that we would lose our spark and our love would suffer.

But this experience has proven very differently. I thought I was satisfied with the way we loved each other before I had cancer, but during this experience, a new type of love has emerged. One that runs deep. One that is based on God and runs on scripture, love, and laughter. One that is totally and completely satisfying.

It is deeper than an outward attraction.

A few days after my surgery, I wanted to take another shower. My friend, who had showered me the first time, was at work, and Luke was the only one available. I told him, "You know I look horrible under these bandages, right? I'm just preparing you." I didn't want him to see my body. But I let go of control and let him see. He just smiled and continued helping me. Once the bandages were removed, and my body which I thought was ruined was revealed, he smiled and said, "I thought you said you looked horrible?" It was then that I realized I was being too hard on myself, and realized how powerful a marriage based on God is. Luke has been so helpful this whole time, from waking up with me at 4 am when I am in pain, to reminding me each night how much he loves me, and that he is proud of me.

I've learned that beauty isn't always on the outside. Yes, I'll lose my hair. Yes, I don't currently recognize my body. But, my marriage is not based on vanity. It is build on God and God says, *"But the Lord said to Samuel, "Do not consider his appearance or his height, for I have rejected him. The Lord does not look at the things people look at. People look at the outward appearance, but the Lord looks at the heart."* 1 Samuel 16:7. On days when I look absolutely horrible, I have confidence knowing that God and my husband love me anyway.

I have written these intimate details because I need you to know that these type of men exist. Do not let the world fool you into settling. The problem is that often we cannot find these types of men because we are too impatient and we settle for the bad boys and the ones we think we can change. My advice to any woman seeking a satisfying love: start with God first.

As women, we desire a love that is based on actions. We set this as the standard for people. You have read about my previous relationships. A common theme in those relationships was that I was constantly told "I love you," but was never shown it. I wanted a love shown with actions.

We desire to be loved with actions, so why then would we think that our love and relationship with God should be any different? Isn't this the most important relationship of all? He gives us everything we need to know about Him through His word. He gives us details about what He likes and what He does not. He tells us specifically what He expects from us. Yet, we assume He will accept just a love expressed with feeling. Scripture shows us over and over that just saying, "I love you, God," with no action behind it is not enough.

Jesus says: "*You shall love the Lord your God with all your heart and with all your soul and with all your mind. This is the great and first commandment.*" Matthew 22:37-38. When I stop and think about my past and the way I displayed love towards God, it makes me shutter. Why did I just tell God I loved Him but did not live like I did? Is it perhaps that we have created our own man made definition of love? Webster's dictionary defines love as: an intense feeling of deep affection. But, it says nothing about action.

The Bible defines love as
"*Love is patient and kind, does not envy or boast; it is not arrogant or rude. It does not insist on its own way; it is not irritable or resentful; it does not rejoice at wrongdoing, but rejoices with the truth. Love bears all things, hopes all things, endures all things. Love never ends.*" (1 Corinthians 13:1-8).. All of these qualities listed are based on action.

So, when I used to say, "I love God," but my actions were saying I was too busy for Him; or I didn't care about reading His word to get to know Him or what He wants for me... Did I really love him? I am not sure I did. Do you know what happens in marriages when people do not demonstrate their love through actions? Or what happens when couples do not take time to pay attention to small details? Those small details add up, and eventually both individuals get fed up with each other. Eventually, it ends in divorce. Assuming that God will just accept a love from me that is not based on action, or that is man made, "an intense feeling of deep affection," terrifies me, because my soul depends on His judgment...I do not want to end up divorced from Him.

He demonstrated His love for us through actions John 3:16

"For God loved the world so much that he gave his one and only Son, so that everyone who believes in him will not perish but have eternal life."

Shouldn't we demonstrate our love for Him in the same way by keeping His commandments?

John 14:15 *"If you love me, you will keep my commandments."*

1 John 4:7-10 - *"Beloved, let us love one another: for love is of God; and every one that loveth is born of God, and knoweth God. He that loveth not knoweth not God; for God is love. In this was manifested the love of God toward us, because that God sent his only begotten Son into the world, that we might live through him. Herein is love, not that we loved God, but that he loved us, and sent his Son to be the propitiation for our sins."*

Yes, I am madly in love with my husband, but the most satisfying love is the one between us and Jesus Christ. It is at our fingertips, but up to us to pursue it.

Thirst Quenching Questions

What does a thirst for love look like in your life?

Jesus says: If you love me, keep my commandments,"
Read John 14:15; in what ways can we keep His commandments?

Read Luke 10:27; in what ways can we love God with our mind?

If your love for God based on your words, or your actions?

What would a love for God based on actions look like in your life?

Read Philippians 2:1-11; what are the qualities of a Christ like love from these verses?

What are some ways we can put these verses into action in every-day life?

Week Ten: Thirsty for Courage

"For God gave us a spirit not of fear but of power and love and self-control." 2 Timothy 1:7

Prior to finding courage from reading God's word, I often sought liquid courage from alcohol. Give me a drink or two, and I felt like I could talk to anyone and do anything. It was unrealistic, dangerous, and I always woke up with a headache. It was a false sense of courage.

When I stopped drinking, I had to find courage elsewhere. Over the past few weeks we have been spending time together delving into moments from my past and into God's word. For a long time, I have been terrified of writing this book. I have been terrified that I would not be able to properly place my thoughts in order or that someone would take something I said the wrong way or hear my writing in the wrong tone. Then I realized that those thoughts are not from God. God does not give us a spirit of fear. I find satisfying courage in the fact that I am using pieces of His words in this book because His words hold so much power.

It is in His word where proper courage can be found. Fear is quite prevalent in my life. The first week of this book I discussed the fact that fear once took over my faith. Even though I am a child of God, I still struggle with fear at times. This journey with cancer has proven to be a fearful time. It is an extremely scary feeling shampooing my hair when I know in a few short weeks I will be bald. It is an even more terrifying feeling when Luke plays with my hair and I love the feeling so much but know it will soon come to an end for a while. I know that it is just hair (I am told this daily). I know that it will grow back. I know that my beauty is not based on my hair, and that being bald will probably be a blessing...I know that I will gain a new strength from being bald and any other encouraging thing someone can possibly say. But I also know that to me, right now, it's not just hair and to someone else experiencing something terrifying, it's not "just" anything. It's another piece of me being removed. It is me losing control of my health and being vulnerable. It is me having to learn how to have inner beauty and not be so focused on my outward appearance. It's me being nervous to be a new bald wife. As well as being nervous to spend the next five months of my life in a chair while chemotherapy infuses into my veins. I experience moments when I completely burst into tears. I also have moments when I am completely annoyed, grumpy, and fearful at this situation. But then I remember that once upon a time, I felt like this when my mom was passing away. During that time, I experienced these same emotions, I thought then that no one knew what I was going through, and felt annoyed when people provided encouraging words. I felt like I was losing control when she died. I was terrified of a future without her.

However, I have come to know that this experience with cancer is not any different than losing my mother, or any other struggle in my Christian walk. There is in fact someone that knows what I am going through, and I do not just mean the sisterhood of breast cancer survivors. (Who by the way, I am extremely thankful for those who have told me their stories and struggles and just say those sweet words "I understand.") There is someone else, who knew what it was like to have this battle with the flesh and He overcame it. It is in Him that my thirst for courage was quenched.

He is the reason that I can courageously write my thoughts in this book and not care that they are not perfectly laid out in order because I know as long as I am trying to give Him glory, He supports me.

God literally spoke us into existence. He left us His words behind in the precious Bible for us to have satisfying courage that He is able to get us through what ever we are going through. If you need a dose of courage right now, I invite you to turn to Mark 14 in your Bible. Read vs 1-9:

"*And while he was at Bethany in the house of Simon the leper, as he was reclining at table, a woman came with an alabaster flask of ointment of pure nard, very costly, and she broke the flask and poured it over his head. There were some who said to themselves indignantly, "Why was the ointment wasted like that? For this ointment could have been sold for more than three hundred denarii and given to the poor." And they scolded her. But Jesus said, "Leave her alone. Why do you trouble her? She has done a beautiful thing to me. For you always have the poor with you, and whenever you want, you can do good for them. But you will not always have me. She has done what she could; she has anointed my body beforehand for burial. And truly, I say to you, wherever the gospel is proclaimed in the whole world, what she has done will be told in memory of her,"* (Mark 14:1-9).

I found courage by reading this passage because of the actions of Mary. Here we see that she was scolded, rebuked, and criticized for her devotion to Jesus (Johnson, 2018). When we love Jesus like Mary did, chances are people will think we are foolish. We will be scolded, rebuked, and most likely criticized. This has proven true in my life. Whether it comes from family or friends or even members in the Lord's church, it happens and will continue to happen. But we need to be like Mary, she did what she could and what was the result? Jesus defended her! He says in vs 6, "*Leave her alone! Why do you trouble her? She has done a beautiful thing to me.*" This gives me so much courage because it shows that when we do what we can for Jesus, He will defend us.

Having a pure devotion to Christ can be intimidating because people often do not respond well. This can often leave us thirsty for courage if we do not satisfy that thirst with reassurance from His word and other Christians.

If we look around the world today we see a wide road that many people are following. It does not take a lot of courage to follow the crowd down this path. In this path of least resistance, people are satisfying their life thirsts with pleasure and comfort, never really feeling fulfilled. I have used this verse many times but it is just so powerful, remember Matthew 7:13-14 Jesus says *"Enter by the narrow gate. For the gate is wide and the way is easy that leads to destruction, and those who enter by it are many. For the gate is narrow and the way is hard that leads to life, and those who find it are few."*

It is so hard to stay on the narrow path. It is lonely on the narrow path and we often times find ourselves vulnerable and out of our comfort zones when we totally devote ourselves to living for Christ. Like Mary, people will question why you are so devoted to the narrow path. But I pray that you stand firm and drink up the courage the written word offers.

In last weeks chapter, we read about a satisfying love. A common belief in our generation is that God is love, so no one will be destroyed. So, they live their lives doing whatever they want to do with no sacrifice. I sometimes do not blame them because sacrificing is hard. Doing God's work is hard. Spending time reading and praying is difficult. Talking to someone about Christ and the gospel is tough. But as God's people, we have to have courage and self discipline to make these sacrifices. Yes God loves us, but He requires obedience.

I am no one's judge, only God can judge. However, I say this is the most *loving* way, God is love, but He is also Just. A glimpse through the Old Testament often makes me tremble. It is a reiteration of how God loves people, yet they constantly turn away from Him. Although they turn away, He is patient for awhile, but eventually takes vengeance. An example of this would be the flood...

Do you realize how many people were saved on the ark during the flood? Only eight!

When I read Matthew 7:21, and I was outside of Christ; it terrified me. I didn't know what the will of God was or if I was following it. I was thirsty for answers, for comfort, for courage to do what is right. Once I was able to look into the Bible and realize that I was able to follow the example laid out for me, it was the most secure feeling. I gained courage when I grounded my faith in the scriptures.

As children of God we can have satisfying courage knowing that we are part of an elect group: *"But you are a chosen race, a royal priesthood, a holy nation, a people for his own possession, that you may proclaim the excellencies of him who called you out of darkness into his marvelous light,"* 1 Peter 2:9

We can work hard and have courage to keep doing the Lord's work because we know that Jesus is coming back. We read these words in 1 Thessalonians 1:7-12
"since indeed God considers it just to repay with affliction those who afflict you, and to grant relief to you who are afflicted as well as to us, when the Lord Jesus is revealed from heaven with his mighty angels in flaming fire, inflicting vengeance on those who do not know God and on those who do not obey the gospel of our Lord Jesus. They will suffer the punishment of eternal destruction, away from the presence of the Lord and from the glory of his might, when he comes on that day to be glorified in his saints, and to be marveled at among all who have believed, because our testimony to you was believed. To this end we always pray for you, that our God may make you worthy of his calling and may fulfill every resolve for good and every work of faith by his power, so that the name of our Lord Jesus may be glorified in you, and you in him, according to the grace of our God and the Lord Jesus Christ."

We can have courage knowing that on this day, we can rejoice because we have followed His gospel and are covered by His blood and know that He will defend us on judgment day; *"And just as it is appointed for man to die once, and after that comes judgment, so Christ, having been offered once to bear the sins of many, will appear a second time, not to deal with sin but to save those who are eagerly waiting for him,"* (Hebrews 9:27).

Thirst Quenching Questions:

Where do you turn for courage?

List some Bible characters who had great courage and tell their story:

Read Psalm 56:3-4; can you confidently proclaim these words? Why or why not?

What types of fear do you struggle with?

Read 2 Timothy 1:7; what type of spirit did God give us?

An old Cherokee once told his grandson "My son, there is a battle between two wolves inside us all. One is evil: anger, jealously, greed, fear, resentment, inferiority, lies, ego.
The other is good: it is joy, peace, love, hope, humility, kindness, empathy, and truth

The boy asked grandfather, "which wolf wins?

The old man quietly replied: " the one you feed."

Which wolf are you feeding?

What does being a courageous Christian, confident in your identity look like in your life?

Week Eleven:- Satisfied

"On the last day of the feast, the great day, Jesus stood up and cried out, "If anyone thirsts, let him come to me and drink. Whoever believes in me, as the Scripture has said, Out of his heart will flow rivers of living water.'" John 7:37

In Nehemiah 8, the book of the law (part of the Bible we know today) was read to the children of Israel (God's chosen people at that time). Scripture says, *"So Ezra the priest brought the Law before the assembly, both men and women and all who could understand what they heard, on the first day of the seventh month. And he read from it facing the square before the Water Gate from early morning until midday, in the presence of the men and the women and those who could understand. And the ears of all the people were attentive to the Book of the Law."* Later in the chapter it says the people mourned and wept after hearing the reading. Over the years they had been led in captivity because they disobeyed God. They sought satisfaction in being disobedient, rebelling against God, casting His law behind their backs, killing prophets who told them what they were doing wrong, and much more (Nehemiah 9:26). But none of that fulfilled them. In fact, it caused them great heartache.

In the book of Jeremiah, the Lord says through Jeremiah, *"for my people have committed two evils: they have forsaken me, the fountain of living waters, and hewed out cisterns for themselves, broken cisterns that can hold no water."* In Bible lands, individuals would dig in the earth and create a space for the collection and storage of water (Biblehistory.com). Since these were man made, they were often broken, and failed to do the job they were designed to do. The Lord compares these broken cisterns to the certain things the people were chasing. The desires they were chasing were never fulfilling. They constantly failed to see that only God could truly fill them.

Both in the book of Jeremiah, and Nehemiah, and constantly written over and over in the scriptures we read of a common theme: people failing to satisfy themselves and always left wanting when they chased worldly pursuits. It was only when they returned to the Lord and His word, that they were properly filled.

As Christians, we are under a new law. Christ abolished the

old law that was established when He was nailed to the cross (Co lossians 2:14). But something has happened today. We have left th Bible behind, and much like the children of Israel, we have create our own gods, and are casting the Bible behind our backs. This i causing us to fail to be properly fulfilled.

Once I decided to open my Bible, I found myself relating t the children of Israel. I once sought satisfaction in everything bu God and following His commandments.

As a teenager, I thought satisfaction would be found in bein accepted by my friends. As an adult, I thought satisfaction woul be found in the perfect boyfriend or perfect career. At times, I eve thought satisfaction would be found at the bottom of a bottle. Bu all those things left me wanting. I felt discontent. I felt as if I wa missing something.

In the beginning of this book, I wrote that I believe that Go has placed a constant thirst in our lives so that we would seek Him I *truly* believe that. I believe those thirsts are a blessing and can hel us turn away from ourselves and back to the one who provides th refreshing solution.

This book may appear as if I am trying to tell you how t live, but I pray that you know that is not my intention. The goa here is to provide you with another option for living. An option o pursuing a *well* that never runs dry. This option is found by turnin back to God's word for fulfillment, getting into Christ, and living life in service to Him.

The feeling of being thirsty can impact each of our lives i many ways. It can cause us to fail to reach our true purpose and fin meaning in life. I hope by sharing my journey you are encourage to examine and share yours and that you experience a satisfyin identity, attention, acceptance, adventure, love, courage, and pur pose.

I am no one special, just a girl with thoughts and experience that have been put on paper in hopes that it would help someone out there find their fullness in God and His word. If this book reaches just one person and makes an impact on your life, I will be happy. I hope that this book has helped you discover your life thirst and I pray that you turn to the One who can quench it.

"Blessed is the man who trusts in the Lord,
And whose hope is the Lord. For he shall be like a tree planted by the waters which spreads out its roots by the river,
And will not fear when heat comes;
But its leaf will be green,
And will not be anxious in the year of drought,
Nor will cease from yielding fruit." Jeremiah 17: 7-9

Thirst Quenching Tips

One approach to Bible study that has helped me tremendously is to approach a passage with questions. I have my husband to thank for teaching me method of study, and I thought that it would benefit you from sharing.

Questions to ask a passage when studying:

1. Who is the author?
2. Who are the readers/listeners?
3. Where is it on the Bible time line?
4. What tools is God or Satan using?
5. What are the roots? Meaning, how does this impact the entire message in the Bible?
6. What other Bible verses relate to this text?
7. How big of a piece of the puzzle is this?

Studying and creating my own Bible time line has also impacted my studies as well, I highly recommend sitting down and creating your own!

Thirst Quenching Resources:

Audio Bible: www.biblegateway.com

Prayer App for Iphone: Echo

Scripture Memorization: www.scripturetyper.com

Suffering: my blog: sorrowfulyetrejoicing.com

Science: Apologeticspress.org

WeeklyVideos: https://www.youtube.com/channel/UCygDFdZnOKlaRmdjHDldcaQ

Bible School: www.worldvideobibleschool.com

References

A General Introduction to the Bible: Lesson 7.(2001).. Apologeticspress. Retrieved from http://apologeticspress.org/pdfs/courses_pdf/hsc0107.pdf

Ancient cisterns. Bible History. Retrieved from https://www.bible-history.com/biblestudy/cisterns.html

Johnson, D. (2018). *Our Sacrificial Love*. Retrieved from https://www.youtube.com/watch?v=Q5RWH8AV3Zc

Harrub, B. (2003). *How did we get the bible?* Apologeticspress.org. Retrieved from
https://www.apologeticspress.org/apcontent.aspx?category=105&article=91

Fransham, J. (2018). *Confessing to one another: The uncomfortable but liberating gift of openness.* Plough Publishing House. Retrieved from https://www.plough.com/en/topics/community/church-community/who-needs-confession

Keathley, J. (2004). *Quenching our thirst at god's fountain.* Bible. Org. Retrieved fromhttps://bible.org/article/quenching-our-thirst-god%E2%80%99s-fountain

McCance, K., Huether, S. (2014). Pathophysiology: The Biologic Basis for Disease in Adults and Children, 7th Edition. [Vitalsource]. Retrieved from https://online.vitalsource.com/#/books/9780323088541/

Moore, J. (2018). *Greek.* World Video Bible School. Retrieved from http://school.wvbs.org/courses/greek/

Mosher,L. (2015). Transformed: A spiritual journey. (2ed.). *World Video Bible School.*

Sin. (2018). Retrieved from https://www.biblestudytools.com/dictionary/sin/

Shank, M. (2011). *Muscle and a shovel*. Retrieved from https://www.michaelshankministries.com/

Shank, M. (2015). *When the shovel breaks.* Retrieved from https://www.michaelshankministries.com/

"Scripture quotations are from The ESV® Bible (The Holy Bible, English Standard Version®), copyright © 2001 by Crossway, a publishing ministry of Good News Publishers. Used by permission. All rights reserved."

Strongs Lexicon. (2018). *Telios.* Blue Letter Bible. Retrieved from https://www. blueletterbible.org/lang/lexicon/lexicon.cfm?t=kjv&strongs=g5046

Thompson, B. (1993). *Biblical accuracy and circumcision on the 8th day.* Apologetics press inc. Retrieved from http://apologeticspress.org/apcontent.aspx?category=13&article=1118

Platt, D. (2015). How to Study the Bible. Secret Church. Retrieved from https://www.youtube.com/results?search_query=david+platt+how+to+study+the+bible

Thirsty.Urbandictionary. Retrieved fromhttps://www.urbandictionary.com/define.php?term=Thirsty

Thirsty.Biblestudytools.com.Retrievedfromhttps://www.biblestudytools.com/search/?s=bibles&q=thirsty&t=niv&c=all